# A Mission Officer Handbook:

## Advancing Catholic Identity and University Mission

## VOLUME ONE

• • •

CreateSpace Independent Publishing Platform

ISBN-13: 978-1494950149
ISBN-10: 1494950146

Association of Catholic Colleges and Universities (ACCU)
One Dupont Circle NW
Suite 650
Washington, DC 20036

http://www.accunet.org

# table of contents

●●●●●●●●●●●●●●●●●●●●●●●

# preface

●●●●●●●●●●●●●●●●●●●●●●

*Michael Galligan-Stierle, Ph.D.*

*A Mission Officer Handbook: Advancing Catholic Identity and University Mission* was created with one goal in mind: Assist all those engaged, especially the mission officer, in strengthening the religious mission of their faith-based institution. More than forty authors and a hundred peer reviewers have contributed to this first volume with this goal in mind.

Advancing Catholic identity and institutional mission in a complex secular world, at a higher education institution that cherishes shared governance, and as part of a faith-based Catholic institution that is ground in a 2000-year-old hierarchical leadership model is a challenging undertaking. Mission officers and those who actively collaborate to advance Catholic higher education in the spirit of *Ex corde Ecclesiae* and its *U.S. Application* asked the Association of Catholic Colleges and Universities to provide resources for their task. This *Handbook* is a response to that plea.

When this project began two years ago, I invited twenty-five of the best and brightest minds within Catholic higher education to each write five pages in the style of *USA Today,* describing a *single aspect* of the mission officer's charge that they had either accomplished or witnessed. The idea was not to construct the ideal mission officer job description, but rather, to advance a best-practice methodology. Once manuscripts arrived and reviewer comments were returned, it became clear that the mission officer reality was significantly broader than I or anyone in the field had realized. Person after person reported successes in aspects of the mission officer's charge that other writers had not captured. Consequently, twenty-five writers turned into eighty contributors, and what was envisioned as a single book has evolved into a two-volume handbook. This is volume I; volume II will be published before the close of 2014.

As the cover of this volume aptly captures, the dimensions of a mission officer's role on campus are diverse, multilayered, and complex. For those readers who may be counting, over sixty roles are identified by the authors included here. Volume II will add to the list of the many hats worn by the mission officer, especially those concerning collaboration with the founding religious community and with the many departments that exist on campus. The challenges encountered by mission officers in these varied roles are just as complex. As Marcheschi and Wiseman keenly observe in an essay within volume I, "Anyone afraid to bleed a little best not apply."

Not satisfied to simply present thoughts written in prose regarding the realities of a mission officer, volume I also offers more than seventy-five best practices sprinkled throughout the essays. This information is listed in sidebars for your convenience. Each identifies where you can locate more details about each of these exemplary programs.

In addition to the authors and reviewers, this *Handbook* has achieved publication because of the perseverance of Janice Bellows Feaman, the assistant on this project. With gentleness and grace she managed the coming and going of edited manuscripts, and oversaw the extraordinary mass of details that are inherent to an endeavor of this size. From beginning to end, it has been a pleasure to work with Janice; all those in Catholic higher education will be eternally grateful for the commitment and excellence that Janice brought to this undertaking.

This book is dedicated to all who have been a part of the first and second waves of mission officers within Catholic higher education. Thank you for your pioneering spirit and your determination to incarnate the best of what Catholic higher education continues to become.

Blessings,
Michael Galligan-Stierle

# introduction

●●●●●●●●●●●●●●●●●●●●●●

**Mission Matters: The Mission Leader – An Innovative Strategy in Catholic Higher Education**

*Michael J. James*
*Oscar Mayorga*
*Joseph J. Lehman, TOR*

Since the promulgation in 1990 of *Ex corde Ecclesiae*, the Apostolic Constitution on Catholic Higher Education, Catholic higher education leaders and their supporting associations have continued to develop a wide range of mission-focused initiatives. Individual campuses and their sponsoring religious communities have increased the profile of their Catholic identity through public conversations, charismatic leadership, curricular development, student formation programming, and participation in nationally sponsored initiatives designed to increase mission leadership capacity. Among the innovative mission strategies being employed across Catholic colleges and universities is the appointment of a senior level mission leader who is expected to provide a comprehensive set of resources across the campus to support the integration of the Catholic mission and the sponsoring religious community's charism.[1]

This chapter is a historical-descriptive narrative of mission leader appointments and key characteristics about these appointees. The selected findings reported in this chapter are taken from a national study of Catholic colleges and universities in the United States conducted in 2010. The full scope of the 2010 study identifies characteristics about mission committees, mission leaders, the administrative units they oversee, the sphere of institutional influence they administer, and the perceptions that mission leaders have about their role and responsibilities.

For this study 139 mission leaders were verified from Catholic colleges and universities in the U.S. and invited to voluntarily participate in the research.[2] Through an analysis of data collected from an online, 64-item survey instrument, and further document

---

1 *A mission leader was defined as someone other than the president who has direct responsibility for the integration of mission across the campus. Mission leaders included a senior administrator of a department or office of mission, and the senior coordinator or chairperson of a campus-wide mission committee.*

2 *Respondents were identified by the Boston College research team through a phone survey and website search process of all of the Catholic colleges and universities in the United States. At the completion of this phase of the research, 139 mission leaders were verified to be employed and active at Catholic higher education institutions—represented across every Carnegie classification of Catholic colleges and universities. In the spring of 2013 this same research team confirmed that an additional 20 senior mission leaders had been established since 2010 with a total of 160 senior mission leaders currently in practice, and this number continues to grow even as this work is being published.*

analysis of mission leaders' curriculum vitae, as well as institutional job descriptions, this study identifies: 1) Who: common mission leader characteristics; 2) What: common characteristics in mission unit structures, strategies, and activities; 3) How: mission leader/unit activities across campus; and 4) Why: common characteristics of and challenges to effective practices in matters of campus-wide mission integration.[3]

Since 1980, when the first senior mission leader was established, the adoption of this mission strategy consistently increased in popularity, but only gradually until 1990. From 1990 to 2010, mission leaders were being appointed at an increasing rate with the most significant expansion occurring between 2006 and 2009. According to the respondents to this research, during the same period (2006–2009) over fifty percent of current mission leaders were appointed to their posts. Over the course of just one academic year, 2008–

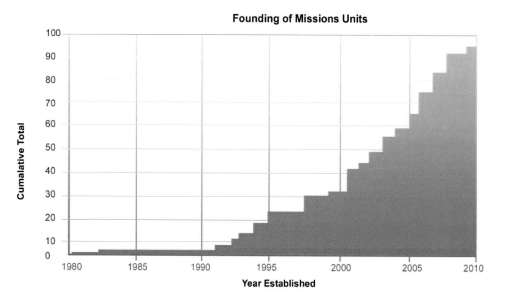

2009, over thirty percent of the 139 mission leaders identified through this study were established.

As the appointment of a mission leader is a relatively recent mission strategy, it is no surprise that over fifty percent of current mission leaders are the first to be appointed to the position at their respective college or university. However, in 2006 the trend in hiring began to replace first-generation mission leaders at an increasing rate with the next generation. Sixty-two percent of current mission leaders hired between 2006 and 2009 were second-generation hires. The increase in the numbers of the next generation of mission leaders is explained by the relatively high age-range of the first-generation mission leaders.

Over seventy percent of mission leaders are members of the college or university founding religious communities. Forty percent are women religious. Thirty-one percent are men religious. Five percent are diocesan priests, and twenty-four percent are lay people. The fact that mission leaders are predominantly made up of senior staff, faculty,

---

3 *Research results are based on a 71 percent survey response rate; 29 percent CV response rate, and 27 percent job description response rate, yielding an overall confidence interval of 95 and a sampling error of 0.*

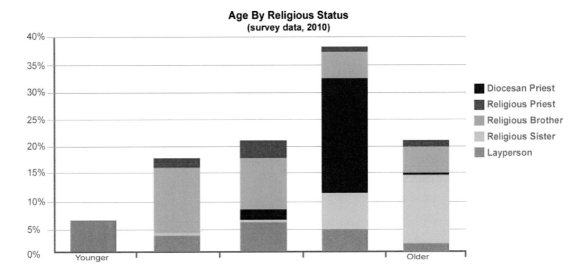

Age By Religious Status
(survey data, 2010)

or administrators from within the institutions' founding religious community is not a surprise. However, if we look at the demographics of the second-generation mission leaders—those hired between 2006 and 2010—a trend appears. The appointments of second-generation mission leaders are increasingly lay people under the age of forty. Prior to 2001 lay people made up only seventeen percent of mission leaders. Between 2001 and 2005 that proportion increased to twenty percent lay people. Mission leader appointments after 2006 increased again to thirty-one percent lay people.

Forty-eight percent of mission leaders serve in another position besides their role as the mission leader. Among those with a joint position, forty-three percent are

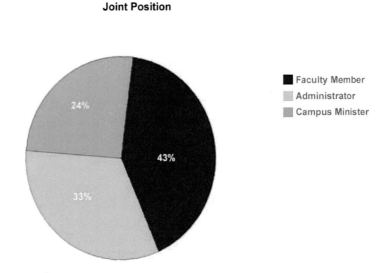

Joint Position

faculty members, one-third are administrators, and one-quarter are campus ministers. Within each of these joint position groups (faculty, administrator, and campus minister) approximately one-half consider their other position to be a dominant responsibility over the mission leader position.

The typical profile for a current mission leader is as follows: white; Catholic; male; over the age of sixty; member of the institution's sponsoring religious community; earned doctorate in a non-theological discipline; served previously as a faculty member, and then in an academic administrative position, or in a leadership position within the sponsoring religious community; and was the first to be appointed as a mission leader. Mission leaders most often describe themselves as a: coordinator; facilitator; collaborator; educator; mentor; animator; catalyst; and a resource person. Mission leaders have extensive experience, knowledge, witness, and passion for the sponsoring community's charism; knowledge of Catholicism, theological training, and familiarity with the Catholic Intellectual Tradition; an ability to successfully work in collaborative situations with a diverse campus community; knowledge of the academic culture and higher education structures; and excellent communication skills.

Over ninety percent of mission leaders responded that they operate with an imperative to give equal attention to both broadly understood Catholic characteristics and distinct charism characteristics in their work. A comprehensive synthesis of the official position descriptions for a mission leader includes the following characteristics: a vice president for mission who assists the president in coordinating, overseeing, and assessing a campus-wide effort to articulate and integrate the mission of the university into the life and ethos of the institution. In keeping with the mission, the position is responsible for the development of programs, initiatives, and activities that both educate and engage students, faculty, administration, staff, board members, alumni, and benefactors in understanding the university's religious identity and commitments. The vice president is particularly attentive to the ways in which the Catholic identity of the university and the spirituality, values, charism, heritage, and educational philosophy of the sponsoring religious congregation are maintained and promoted, while remaining inclusive and accessible to people from other faith traditions and diverse backgrounds.

The descriptive data and analysis of the findings from the first phase of this research advance the following questions: How might campus leaders make informed decisions about implementing mission-related strategies? Does the appointment of a mission leader build mission-capacity on a college or university campus? Is this strategy an appropriate investment in time, talent, personnel, and financial resources? How might competent mission leaders be identified and selected? How is the effectiveness of mission leaders and their programs measured? How might reliable methods of assessment be developed? The relevance of this research will be measured by the degree to which the findings inform constructive answers to these questions.

*Michael J. James is Lecturer, Department of Educational Leadership & Higher Education, and Director of the Institute for Administrators in Catholic Higher Education, Boston College, Boston, MA.*

*Oscar J. Mayorga is a Research and Diversity Consultant, Boston, MA.*

*Rev. Joseph J. Lehman, TOR is Director of Mission Integration at Saint Francis University, Loretto, PA.*

## section ONE
• • • • • •

### Creating a Mission Culture in the Catholic University

## chapter ONE

## Catholic Higher Education and Campus Culture: The Relationship of the Founding Charism and a Church in Service to Others

### Barbara Humphrey McCrabb

*Ex corde Ecclesiae* and *The Application of Ex corde Ecclesiae for the United States* provide a framework for Catholic higher education that affords each campus the opportunity to express principles and norms according to its unique institutional purpose. The mission officer contributes to his or her institution by knowing and appropriating *Ex corde Ecclesiae* and *The Application of Ex corde Ecclesiae for the United States*. The challenge of today's mission officer is to empower the campus community to live its Catholic identity in relationship with the Catholic Church.

*Ex corde Ecclesiae*, a 1990 apostolic exhortation by Pope John Paul II, describes what it means to be a Catholic university. Recognizing similarities among Catholic universities, *Ex corde Ecclesiae* acknowledges as the cornerstone: the quest for truth and the education of individuals for service to Church and society (31-37). Pope John Paul II articulates four essential characteristics of Catholic identity: Christian inspiration, reflection in the light of faith upon the growing treasury of human knowledge, fidelity to the Christian message, and service to the people of God (13).

Reflecting the American context of Catholic higher education, the U.S. bishops outlined their implementation plan in the 2000 document, *The Application of Ex corde Ecclesiae for the United States*. Building on the foundational characteristics, the bishops pointed to the university's commitment to Catholic ideals, principles, and attitudes in carrying out research, teaching, and all other activities (*Application*, Part I, 7.6) while creating a campus culture that both expresses and supports a Catholic way of life (*Application*, Part I, 7.12). The bishops call upon administrators and teachers to serve as role models, indeed as living witnesses to the Catholic faith (*Application*, Part I, 7.8).

Pope Benedict XVI, during his 2008 visit, addressed Catholic educators, expressing his belief that Catholic identity does not depend on statistics—the number of Catholics enrolled, Masses celebrated, or crucifixes hanging on the wall. Nor can Catholic identity simply be equated with the orthodoxy of course content. Instead, he envisioned a distinctive Catholic identity emerging from a living, breathing reality that permeates a Catholic campus.

One way to acknowledge Catholic identity arises from celebrating the charism of the sponsoring congregation. Described as a gift of the Holy Spirit, charism becomes recognized and emulated by others. Inspired by the Holy Spirit, women and men throughout history have set out on a mission to make the gift visible and concrete in the world. One charism encourages care for the poor, another leads to teaching women life skills, and still another prompts a response to health care needs. While the task varies from person to person based on the call they received, the mission remains the same: serving all God's people. Some of these holy men and women, or their followers, institutionalize their gift through Catholic higher education.

Just as religious communities embody the charism of their founder or foundress, similarly Catholic colleges seek to exemplify

Service Programs

• University members serve in diocesan ministries: after-school programs, reading programs, elder care, meal programs, homeless shelters, HIV support, and disability services.
• Teacher Corp recruits recent graduates to serve for two years as teachers in Catholic elementary schools in the diocese.
• Senior administrator advises the diocese on forming a Catholic school board.

their distinctive character. Stories celebrating the charism's reception and embodiment make the founder and the gift accessible to people of all faith traditions. It's true that Saint Francis, the venerable Catherine McCauley, or Saint Benedict do not physically walk today's campus. It is also true that mission-driven community members personify the gift and advance the founders' worldview. The mission officer and all mission activators, rooted in the Holy Spirit and life of the Church, bring the charism to life in tangible ways.

The mission officer, endeavoring to highlight the school's Catholic identity, must know and personally appropriate the charism of the founder or foundress. While entrusted to the entire university community, the gift depends upon those designated with mission responsibility to pursue the mission by engaging the community. The mission officer assists the campus community in appropriating the charism through: study of *Ex corde Ecclesiae*, *The Application of Ex corde Ecclesiae for the United States*, and institutional documents, review of the charism for congruence with the mission and campus activities, contemporary adaptation, and intentional embodiment. Affirming the gift of the Spirit wherever it takes root and nourishing small initiatives where it has yet to blossom, the mission officer serves as a catalyst fostering Catholic identity in support of the university's mission.

The 2011 ten-year review of *The Application of Ex corde Ecclesiae for the United States*, conducted by the United States Conference of Catholic Bishops, featured conversations between bishops and presidents on the local level and regional discussions among bishops at the General Assembly. The final report reflects a prevailing positive tone among them. The Committee on Catholic Education recommended continued dialogue between bishops and presidents, attention to hiring for mission, formation for trustees, faculty, and staff regarding Catholic identity, and addressing the need for improved, accurate, and deeper theological and catechetical knowledge through curricular and pastoral means.

Relationship with the Church, the experience of communion, endures at the heart of a distinctively Catholic identity. This connection operates universally and locally, most visibly demonstrated in the rapport between the local bishop and the president. Pope John Paul II depicts this relationship as one of *mutual trust, close and consistent cooperation, and continuing dialogue*, where bishops participate in the life of the university (*Ex corde Ecclesiae*, 28). Affirming the importance of this relationship the U.S. bishops, in their *Application of Ex corde*

*Ecclesiae for the United States,* emphasized each aspect (*Application*, Part 1, 4.6). Trust rooted in shared baptismal belief provides a foundation for personal and pastoral relations. Cooperation stems from a common effort toward a shared goal that reflects an integration of faith and reason. Dialogue provides a forum for conversation that allows the relationship to flourish over time.

Relationships, on- and off-campus, remain integral to the role and responsibility of the mission officer. *Ex corde Ecclesiae* emphasized the university's essential relationship with

### Educational Opportunities

• Offer undergraduate, graduate, and continuing education courses as well as virtual or online learning in light of diocesan needs.
• Train teachers, principals, catechists, lay ministers, priests, deacons, and religious.
• Develop particular curriculum: lay formation, priestly formation, Hispanic ministry, and leadership development for teachers wanting to become principals.

the Catholic Church, personified primarily through the interaction between the bishop and the president. The mission officer and sometimes board chair support the president by advancing connections through the pursuit of common interests, collaborative projects, and potential areas of service. The success of Church relations, for the mission officer, hinges upon dynamic and supportive relationships among the campus community and with the diocese.

The mutual trust stressed by Pope John Paul comes from shared beliefs. Not long ago most presidents at Catholic colleges were predominantly priests or religious who not only shared baptismal beliefs, but similar formation experiences as well. Today one cannot assume shared belief or similar formation. The president, often with assistance from the mission officer, fosters communication by finding formal and informal ways to get to know the bishop and other key diocesan leaders. By affirming shared beliefs and common values where they exist, the mission officer makes valuable connections that foster trust. Regular contact and informational updates strengthen the working relationship.

Amidst this ongoing relationship, the mission officer,

The bishop...
• hosts small groups of faculty or senior administrators for a monthly/bi-annual lunch.
• gathers presidents of his diocese to discuss mutual concerns of the universities and the diocese.
• sets up with the university mutually agreeable times and occasions when he can come to campus to formally and informally engage.

The president...
• invites the bishop to regular (monthly, quarterly, annual) campus events using different venues such as formal meetings, dinners with no agenda, athletic events, and campus programs.
•sends a letter to the bishop introducing new theology faculty.
• alternates with the bishop in hosting a conversation with the theology faculty to discuss contemporary theological issues twice a year.

## Collaborative Initiatives

• A Catholic medical center, a Catholic university, and Catholic Charities create a holistic child care and early development center.

• The university contributes content and personnel to the diocesan mission which addresses racism and poverty through the Urban Faith Roundtable.

• Drawing upon the university's expertise, a pastoral letter blends Gospel values with environmental concerns.

• The bishop and diocese assist in the university's capital campaign.

• • • • • • • • • • • • • • • • • • • • • • • • • • • • • • • • • •

with knowledge of campus capabilities and diocesan concerns, can facilitate interaction between the university and the diocese. The mission officer promotes collaboration by encouraging conversation between particular campus and diocesan personnel, which leads to mutually beneficial results. Experiences articulated by bishops and presidents in *Promising Practices: Collaboration Among Catholic Bishops and University Presidents* (Galligan-Stierle, 2005) offer models for communication and collaboration.

By acknowledging distinctive roles and appreciating particular responsibilities of both president and bishop, the mission officer helps nurture the relationship. Cultivating respect further enriches the university-diocesan connection. The promotion of genuine dialogue and sacred listening between the Church, with a long tradition of seeking truth, and the university, with a desire for knowledge and dedication to the intellectual life, reinforces and enhances the relationship. Furthermore, as Catholic universities become increasingly diverse, the mission officer can boost Church relations by encouraging ecumenical and interfaith discussion on campus.

Through the framework of *Ex corde Ecclesiae* and *The Application of Ex corde Ecclesiae for the United States*, every campus comes to realize the constitutive nature of Catholic identity and relationship with the Church. A successful mission officer addresses the task at hand with creative engagement of the entire campus community. Through deliberation and discernment, as well as consultation and training, the campus community will grow toward an intentional and enthusiastic embrace of their Catholic identity, in and through the Church in service to others.

*Barbara H. McCrabb is Assistant Director for Higher Education, Secretariat of Catholic Education, United States Conference of Catholic Bishops, Washington, DC.*

## chapter TWO

**It Takes a Village: Creating and Sustaining a Mission-Oriented Culture at a College or University**

*Catherine McMahon, RSM*

"It takes a village" to create and sustain a mission-oriented culture on a college or university campus. Whether you think of Hillary Clinton, Jane Cohen-Fletcher, or African tribal wisdom when you hear that opening, the message nonetheless suggests that mission belongs to the community, not to any one person or office. As the role of the mission officer continues to unfold and become integral to the infrastructure of Catholic colleges and universities, it is important to remember this. Yes, a mission officer can facilitate and coordinate, suggest and influence, but ultimately the success of mission integration depends on the community that embodies it. This essay summarizes one campus community's multidimensional strategies to create and sustain a vibrant, mission-driven approach to its common vision of "preparing distinctive Mercy graduates."

Every sector of the institution must be involved in mission orientation and formation, and in dialogue about the relevance and importance of mission, not only to that sector but to the entire enterprise. "Distinctive Mercy graduates" can only be prepared by a community that prepares itself to be distinctively Mercy and that inculcates that ethos in all dimensions of the students' experience. All members of the community will be involved in mission at a variety of levels and with various levels of commitment, from orientation to formation to appropriation, integration, and application. The role of the mission officer is to provide opportunities and guidance for all levels of engagement and commitment from orientation throughout the student's attendance or the employee's time at the university.

## Orientation

Students are introduced to mission at the yearly welcome weekend with specific programs and an initial service project that includes reflection on mission and Mercy. The core curriculum, freshman year experience (FYE), and signature courses are intended to provide ongoing orientation to mission and values, including a required service component in the FYE course. Alternative break trips are planned as immersion/service experiences and most often are offered at sites where Mercy is present.

Orienting employees begins before they are hired. Hiring for mission includes reflection materials for search committees and candidates in the hiring process, orientation process and materials, tools for performance review, and suggestions for ongoing mission formation. The Office of Mission and Planning conducts/sponsors the new faculty, administrators,

*Commitment to Community* (C2C) is a document that articulates Catholic and Marianist values and serves as an introduction to the University of Dayton's student handbook. C2C enables students to understand principles of community living and develop habits for responsible living aligned with the Catholic and Marianist values of human dignity and the common good.

• • • • • • • • • • • • • • • • • • • • • • • • • • • • • • • •

and staff two-hour required mission orientation, which includes a history of the Sisters of Mercy and of the college, and discussion of the mission and core values.

Trustee orientation to mission, designed by the president, chair, and mission officer, is delivered in one half-day session to new board members, and during yearly day-long retreats for all board members. Beginning board meetings with short prayer services helps to immerse trustees' stewardship and commitment in the spiritual worldview of the university's educational mission.

## Formation

The Mission and Values Committee (M&VC), a standing committee that reports to the special assistant to the president who also functions as the mission officer, guides several formational activities throughout the year. Charged to be "conveners of the dialogue" related to the mission and core values of the college, the M&VC provides forums and presents programs throughout the year related to mission integration. An effective program has been the *Annual Mission Theme*. Each year the M&VC chooses a theme related to one or two of the core values or something that has been highlighted by the sponsors such as the *Critical Concerns of Mercy*. Faculty then incorporate this into their syllabi for the year, and co-curricular programs are focused on the theme. For example, the library committee collaborates by choosing the "Gwynedd Reads" program with the mission theme in mind.

Some employees engage more intensively in mission-related activities at the university. These individuals are invited to join the *Mission Leadership Academy* (MLA). Designed in three levels to permit "members" to commit more deeply, depending on their time and interests, this substantive formation program empowers faculty and staff to become mission animators within the community.

A comprehensive mission orientation, in the form of a yearlong seminar series, is offered to new faculty at Notre Dame of Maryland University. Each month faculty from all schools and departments meet, and a different theme is introduced. The program invites a shared perspective and commitment, building unity among new and current faculty.

• • • • • • • • • • • • • • • • • • • • • • • • • • • • • • • •

A weeklong celebration known as *Mercy Week* is held in late September. It includes programs related to the heritage of the sponsoring community, as well as mission-related current topics, such as election year preparation in light of Catholic Social Teaching, faithful citizenship, common ground, etc.

Liturgy is celebrated daily and for special occasions. It invites the community into the experience of the most sacred mystery of a Catholic institution. Prayer, retreats, and reflections are designed to further illuminate the richness of Catholic and Mercy identity and values.

The yearly performance review process is designed to invite employees and managers to reflect on individual contributions to the community. Each year individuals are encouraged to assess themselves on how they have contributed to the identity, mission, and values of the university.

## Appropriation and Integration

The General Education Curriculum, including Freshman Year Experience, *Signature* and capstone courses, as well as courses with service-learning, all include elements of mission that are designed to challenge students to engage more fully in society and to invite reflection on social responsibility and authentic citizenship.

Students become substantively engaged as community leaders by participation in co-curricular leadership programs and service opportunities available through campus ministry, clubs and organizations, resident life and athletics. These student opportunities are designed to complement curricular offerings, as well as to provide ways for faculty and staff to model service and leadership.

For faculty the *Mission Development Program* (MDP) is the second level of the MLA in which some "members" choose to become "scholars" by participating in an eighteen-month program of study in Catholic theology and social teaching, Mercy heritage, and the "critical concerns" of Mercy. This program was designed by the Conference for Mercy Higher Education (CMHE) and adapted for use on this campus.

## Application

Faculty who complete the MDP are expected to further incorporate mission-related material into their syllabi and to explore ways that service-learning can enhance their pedagogy and the engagement of students in their call to become "distinctively Mercy."

The final stage of the MLA invites faculty and staff mission leaders to share their understanding and commitment to mission through presentations at professional gatherings, participation in mission-related experiences with students and colleagues, mentoring newer faculty and staff, and implementing orientation experiences for new students, faculty, and staff. Each scholar engages an integration project either as an

Integrating Catholic identity with student conduct at St. Catherine University allows students to experience firsthand the concepts of reason, human dignity, community, inclusivity, rights and responsibilities, and social justice. Conduct meetings are formatted on the Pastoral Circle model, which allows students to explore the incident, reflect on the experience, analyze the circumstances, assess their involvement, and collaborate with the hearing officer to create a plan to move forward.

individual or as a team member. For some, these projects include immersion experiences or new ways to approach a particular course or program. Grant writing for mission activities, online programs, and heritage videos are additional examples of integration projects. Two members attend and present at the Carlow Round Table in Ireland with other Mercy colleagues to consider and share the influence of Mercy and Catholic Social Teaching on their particular work at the college. All scholars replace themselves in the Academy so as to sustain the program and broaden the sphere of influence.

## Conclusion

So while a mission officer can and does play a key role in this process of mission sustainability, the village that is the college community is the ground upon which mission is sown and tended and where it ultimately grows and blooms in each generation. It takes a community that knows, understands, values, and engages its mission in every aspect of the institution. It takes a commitment of resources and intention at every level, in every department, division, and school. It takes strong leadership from the trustees through the administration, through management, and by the faculty and staff. And in this case, it also invites a core community of colleagues and students who choose to be mission leaders and who will challenge one another and the "village" in the efforts to co-create and sustain the mission and identity of the institution. Each college or university will approach this challenge from its own charism and its own culture, but each institution will be successful only if it engages and encourages everyone to contribute to the best of his or her ability and trusts that the God who has begun this great good work of Catholic education will see it to completion.

*Sr. Catherine McMahon, RSM is Special Assistant to the President for Mission and Planning, Gwynedd Mercy University, Gwynedd Valley, PA.*

## chapter THREE

## The Mission Officer: Employing Community Organizational Strategies

*Mary Beth Gallagher*

Imagine a community organizer dressed in a T-shirt, flip-flops, and jeans, smoking a cigarette and using salty language while plotting an activity over a few beers in a bar. Now, contrast the mission officer, a woman of a certain age, wearing suit or jacket, speaking earnestly about a faculty retreat over coffee in a small, unassuming conference room on campus. These opposing stereotypes reflect two occupations with remarkable similarities. Both leaders:

- Are clear about the goals they wish to accomplish;
- Use strategic collaboration to get things done;
- Depend on strong, volunteer leaders to support their programs financially and in terms of popular "buy-in";
- Succeed by knowing the priorities and skills of their constituents.

A fundamental insight the community organizer can offer the mission officer is to learn the true motives and passions of those within his or her organization. What excites them? Some people exhibit little zest for anything, and a few may share areas of interest that don't initially appear useful. The mission officer willing to dig deeper may unearth a different reality. The daily practice of engaging new and existing members of the college community in brief conversation is an excellent means of discovering where the "fire in their bellies" lies. In this way the mission officer begins to learn the priorities and values of the community.

"…All of us are asked to obey his call to go forth from our own comfort zone in order to reach all the 'peripheries' in need of the light of the Gospel." (*Evangelii Gaudium*, 20)

The task of initiating so many conversations may daunt the new mission officer; seasoned veterans may believe they already know enough about the people in their community. But what animates an individual can change over time. It is the mission officer's current knowledge of his or her constituents that becomes the shortcut needed for such a task. Engaging in short, daily conversation with members of the community takes less time than one might imagine.

What does this shortcut look like? It involves brief, focused conversations with many people. When talking with someone new, the mission officer seeks to understand the people, values, and practices that motivate that individual. Asking easily answered questions and freely sharing hope-filled personal information often helps to build a positive relationship. The departmental chairperson might seem principally concerned with her research agenda, while in reality it may be her autistic teenager who holds her energy and attention. The Muslim faith of the food service employee may be what brings life to his day.

As mission officers converse with people, they understand the importance of setting aside preconceptions concerning what drives an individual. People are full of surprises. One way to learn about others is to invite them to share about their favorites, e.g., favorite class, teacher, leisure activity, or characteristic of the school. The professor of literature may be more enthusiastic about recruiting high-achieving students to campus than about teaching or research. The vice president may care little about "looking successful," and instead have a powerful desire to serve at a Catholic institution. Using the principle of "following the energy," the mission officer discovers the key issues driving an individual, whether those issues relate to work or home. Recording key information about people enables the mission officer to engage new, energetic contributors to mission efforts.

Mission-centric recruitment events at Mount St. Mary's involve the entire community. Administrators, faculty, staff, and students assist the Admissions Office in over seventy recruitment presentations each year. Speakers incorporate the university's mission and Catholic identity into presentations about their specific area of expertise, better equipping all staff members to talk about the mission and university as a whole.

"Power conversations" can make an exciting contribution to the mission officer's work. For example, a mission officer wanting to plan a speaker series on Catholic Social Teaching would work with a committee. The program, through the committee, immediately gains additional commitment. The committee will not reduce the mission officer's workload. In fact it will require more work than completing the tasks alone, but an engaged committee will spread the mission's message widely and more effectively. Ideally, the diversity of the committee opens the mission officer to new insights into others' views of mission programming. After a number of conversations on campus, the mission officer may find the committee consists of:

- A chemistry faculty member who works with his Jewish synagogue's food pantry;
- A student group eager to share the story of their summer service in Africa;
- A social work faculty member who sees the overlap between the purposes of social work and Catholic Social Teaching;
- The new president of the University Staff Association who would like to reactivate the organization after a few years of low activity;
- An accounting faculty member, with a small group of interested accounting majors, who believes "we don't have enough interdisciplinary colloquia on campus."

The mission officer gathers together these unlike companions and presents the concept and some options for the speaker series—not a fully formed plan. Bringing ideas and energy, the mission officer asks for advice regarding content, format, and logistics. Everyone present, even if they are unacquainted with each other, is an energetic stakeholder for unique reasons.

This recruiting process, based on power conversations, differs sharply from issuing a general call for volunteers. Community organizers consider a broad invitation for volunteers to be bad practice because the volunteers (who can be difficult to dismiss) may not have the skills or motives needed for the task at hand. Contrast that practice (of taking whomever responds) with inviting someone known to have the skills needed: "Keara, you're the best person I know to develop the new webpage with the Undergraduate Curriculum Committee. I know that you can do this…. Are you willing to help advance the college mission in this way?" The high rate of positive responses to such invitations may shock the mission officer familiar with making requests from overworked colleagues. When people see that the mission officer recognizes and values their capabilities, they are more inclined to help.

The mission officer needs to be wary of judging what others value, and cautious to avoid sentimental expectations. Some staff do not support the president, and some faculty don't enjoy teaching. Tapping into what *truly* excites someone—community organizers call it an individual's "self-interest"—adds motivation and vitality. Arm twisting isn't necessary to persuade people to attend a meeting where their interests will be addressed and their goals accomplished.

Conceiving of the mission officer as a community organizer suggests some powerful tools for enlivening the mission on campus. The community organizer-turned-mission officer will know how to identify, empower, and support people who implement mission activities on their own. He or she will be able to build excitement around mission activities in new ways, bump up participation in mission programs, and finally avoid the trap of asking for volunteers—while continuously refreshing mission activities with energetic contributions from a growing community.

*Mary Beth Gallagher is Assistant to the President for Mission Integration, Fontbonne University, St. Louis, MO.*

## chapter FOUR

## Creating and Strengthening a Campus-Wide Mission Effectiveness Committee

*Lois Sculco, SC*

The year 2012 marked the 50th anniversary of the opening of the Second Vatican Council. This historic event of the Catholic Church urged a new understanding of other faith traditions, broadened the role of laity as collaborators in church work, and invited people of good will to work together in the transformation of society. This significant event in the life of the Church has had the fortunate byproduct of encouraging Catholic institutions to explore what it means to embrace Catholic identity and to engage in Catholic mission activities within a pluralistic culture and interfaith religious landscape. This brief chapter will highlight how Catholic institutions can more effectively embrace these Vatican II concepts through the sustained efforts of a mission and identity committee.

"A Catholic University must become more attentive to the cultures of the world today, and to the various cultural traditions existing within the Church in a way that will promote a continuous and profitable dialogue between the Gospel and modern society." (*Ex corde Ecclesiae*, 45)

An effective mission officer today acknowledges the multiple gifts of the university community when he or she creates a representational campus-wide advisory committee to serve with the mission officer. Collaborating with the mission officer, the campus-wide mission and identity committee brings synergy to the ongoing work of strengthening the Catholic identity of the university. Ownership of the university, in the spirit of the Second Vatican Council, increases in proportion to members of the community taking responsibility for the institution's Catholic identity and educational mission. This committee's responsibility remains constant even though the membership of the Mission and Identity Committee will change from time to time. The president originally appoints the members and explains the committee's purpose. Additions and replacements are made by the mission officer, by volunteer members, and by Senate appointments.

The committee's programming is strengthened and the mission of the university advanced when the conversation expands past the committee members to include faculty, professional staff, operational staff, students, and trustees. At Seton Hill University, the committee established four task forces. Each task force focuses on the charism of the sponsoring congregation and the academic core of teaching and scholarship in the following four ways: Welcoming, Celebrating, Learning, and Serving. The ongoing activities of each task force help the Catholic identity flourish.

The success of the Mission and Identity Committee and the four task forces is directly related to the commitment of those involved and the monies provided by the university to advance the different initiatives. While there are many committee initiatives that can be found on the Seton Hill website, a few examples follow:

- Grant money is available to assist in the study of Church documents. The committee can read, discuss, and reflect on a document and then invite a speaker such as the local bishop or president of the sponsoring congregation.
- The group may have a "study year," looking at Church documents such as *Gaudium et Spes*, or *We Remember: A Reflection in the Shoah*.
- The committee can choose to publish a university document that would connect its work with the culture and traditions of the institution, the four characteristics of Catholic identity identified in *Ex corde Ecclesiae*, and the charism of the sponsoring congregation. Thus, the Seton Hill University Catholic Identity document was developed and is revised annually.
- Companion documents can be revised and published, such as the *Principles of Good Practice for Student Affairs at Catholic Colleges and Universities*, found at www.accunet.org.
- In addition to these initiatives, the creativity of the four committees can advance additional programs:
  - The Welcoming Task Force uses the Seton Hill University Catholic Identity booklet and other materials to orient all new employees, new trustees, and new students and their families to the history and mission of the university. The Seton Hill University Catholic Identity booklet includes some university pictures and quotes from the following sources: *Ex corde Ecclesiae*, Elizabeth Ann Seton, the president of the university, and students. A faculty member and the mission officer orient all new faculty members in a three-hour session including both the Catholic identity and liberal arts mission, indicating that relationship and using handouts on Catholic Social Teaching, Distinguishing Characteristics of Catholic Intellectual Tradition, and case studies. The mission officer orients new trustees and new students and their families. Members of the committee orient other new employees in their areas. The committee members use the Seton Hill University Catholic Identity booklet and other materials that are appropriate to the group. New Student Life employees also use the *Principles* document. Each session is about one or two hours.

    "The front door, the back door, the side door that leads to the Chapel...all the windows, upstairs and downstairs, open at your coming." (Saint Elizabeth Ann Seton)

  - The Celebrating Task Force builds community by planning Roman Catholic and interfaith and ecumenical liturgical services, including Kristallnacht and Yom HaShoah in cooperation with the National Catholic Center for Holocaust Education. This group also celebrates annually a special event titled "Lunch with Liz." Each year the group celebrates the life of Elizabeth Ann Seton in a variety of creative ways, honoring students who have Sisters of Charity Scholarships and highlighting Sister of Charity pioneers for whom the scholarships are named.

"The Gospel...constantly invites us to rejoice.... Why should we not also enter into this great stream of joy?" (*Evangelii Gaudium,* 5)

• • • • • • • • • • • • • • • • • • • • • • • • • • • •

• The Learning Task Force has, in recent years, promoted three summer workshops, conducted by Barbara Wall, for faculty who then incorporate the principles of CST into the core curriculum and major fields. Twenty-two faculty members have revised major courses to include these principles. This task force has assessed CST in the curriculum. Members of this task force also include the staff of the National Catholic Center for Holocaust Education. The center annually programs internal events and triennially conducts the Ethel LaFrak Holocaust Education Conference (DelDuca, 2011). This links our Catholic Identity booklet to the work of the center.

• The Serving Task Force coordinates many service activities such as Habitat for Humanity, Labor of Love in September, Take the Day On, Martin Luther King Jr., Day, and service activities for agencies in the local community through the year. This task force identifies all service projects as part of campus ministry programming, academic department programming, and athletic service projects. These service opportunities are part of the CST initiative, and members explore different ways in which students, staff, and faculty can gain global awareness, respect for diversity, and love of creation as ways to transform the world.

"Directors and administrators in a Catholic university promote the constant growth of the university and its community through a leadership of service; the dedication and witness of the non-academic staff are vital for the identity and life of the University." (*Ex corde Ecclesiae,* 24)

• • • • • • • • • • • • • • • • • • • • • • • • • • • •

## Conclusion

In the spirit of the Second Vatican Council, mission officers continue to strengthen the Catholic mission and identity of the institution. A campus-wide committee, comprised of various task forces, can foster campus-wide collaborations and energize the Mission Office in meeting new challenges with passion and dedication.

*Sr. Lois Sculco, SC is Vice President for Institutional Identity, Mission, and Student Life at Seton Hill University, Greensburg, PA.*

---

*Reference*
DelDuca, G. (2011). "Teaching the Holocaust as Part of a University's Catholic Identity." *Journal of Catholic Higher Education*, 30:2, 199-220.

## chapter FIVE

**Advancing the Institutional Catholic Story through Art, Symbolism, and Architecture**

*Kurt Schackmuth*

The mission officer is a storyteller: a resource and expert on the institution's Catholic identity, the story of the sponsoring religious order, and the heritage and traditions of the college. The mission officer is also a creative individual, an "idea person," someone who is always looking for the next best way to advance the mission. He or she must have confidence, enthusiasm, and energy for this work and be willing to advocate for his or her ideas.

One way to communicate the mission is through the use of art, symbolism, and campus architecture. These approaches can have a significant impact on the campus population and are easier to implement than one would first imagine. They shouldn't be overlooked as a viable means for communicating the primacy of the college or university's mission and Catholic identity. Here are some common examples:

- *Adopt a uniform standard crucifix, or display a diverse selection of crucifixes across campus.* A beginning goal could be to display a crucifix in every building on campus, leading to additional crucifixes in various rooms. Church supply catalogs are a good place to start. Also consider asking faculty, staff, and students who travel outside the country to bring back unique religious art pieces.

- *Design a standardized depiction of the college's mission statement for display in key locations and buildings around campus.* A framed and matted version of the mission statement will work just fine, or consider a museum-style exhibit panel that depicts the mission statement and an image of the founder of the sponsoring religious order. Include additional photos, descriptions of core values, or significant quotations in the exhibit.

- *Hang religiously inspired artwork in hallways and other public spaces on campus.* Religious art brings to mind priceless masterworks hanging in a museum. However, it is not necessary to spend tremendous amounts of money on high-end, original art pieces. Consider framing and matting full-color prints or reproductions. Religious art can be images of holy men and women, saints, historical figures, traditional iconography, or inspirational Bible passages or quotations. For example, artist John August Swanson offers a beautiful selection of prints that depict Bible stories from his original serigraphs. Consider commissioning an original piece of art by a faculty member from the art department or creating a student competition complete with campus displays and a cash award for students. Statues, inside and outside, sculptures, and stained glass are other good options. Remember, religious art need not be limited to display in the campus chapel.

- *Display images related to the founding charism or religious order.* There are significant men and women among founding religious orders who inspire and deserve to be remembered. Their stories are worth telling! Consider displaying images of these individuals, along with brief biographical sketches, on campus where various constituencies will have access to them.

- *Develop a historical timeline wall display of the college's story.* Feature brief stories, photographs, and graphics that reflect the institution's Catholic roots and/or the founding religious order. Museum-quality panels and exhibit materials are easy to obtain and relatively inexpensive to develop. Wall murals are another great way to communicate the institutional story. Encourage admission office staff to stop at the timeline during campus tours with prospective students to learn about the mission of the college and key elements of the institution's Catholic identity. Invite current students to refresh the display to keep it visually appealing.

- *Name public spaces, meeting rooms, residence halls, or buildings that reflect elements of the college's mission.* Many institutions name buildings and spaces on campus for donors and friends who helped build them. Consider naming buildings in the spirit of the mission, honoring Catholic saints, prominent individuals from the Catholic Intellectual Tradition, and significant individuals from the founding congregation's tradition. Plaques and photos can feature information about the name given to the building.

  Lewis University (Romeoville, IL) has residence halls named after Pope John Paul II, Mother Teresa, and Dorothy Day, as well as other buildings on campus named after the institution's founders. Lewis also has several buildings and spaces named after specific De La Salle Christian Brothers who had lasting impacts on campus.

- *Construct a grotto, labyrinth, or exterior "sacred space" for reflection and prayer.* Providing spaces on campus for faculty, staff, and students to develop their spirituality and enhance faith development is important. Contemplative areas such as labyrinths, fountains, gardens, grottos, and prayer spaces with statues, benches, chimes, reflecting pools, and crosses or crucifixes can all enhance how one experiences the mission on the campus.

The projects mentioned above can be accomplished through hard work, advocacy, planning, creativity, and of course, funding. It is appropriate for the mission officer to take the lead in implementing these projects and initiatives in collaboration with others on campus. Remember, the mission officer must be a creative idea person, an advocate for Catholic identity (and the sponsoring charism, if there is one), as well as a project manager and an organizer. He or she must constantly be thinking of new ways to communicate the mission, and help deepen understanding of it among members of the college community. It takes relationships, funding, and structures to make these projects happen.

## Relationships

The mission officer must develop and cultivate relationships among the campus community. It's important for the mission officer to be known and respected in a variety of circles. Faculty, staff, and administrators should know that the mission officer is a resource and an advocate for advancing the mission—someone who is open to the ideas of others and willing to listen to suggestions for enhancing the integration of mission into all areas of campus. It is just as important for the mission officer to be known by employees in the president's office, campus ministry, human resources, academic affairs, and student development, as it is to be known to those in the admissions office, institutional advancement, academic departments, campus police, athletics, satellite campus directors, and the maintenance department.

---

"When we adopt a pastoral goal and a missionary style which would actually reach everyone without exception or exclusion, the message has to concentrate on the essentials, on what is most beautiful, most grand, most appealing and at the same time most necessary." (*Evangelii Gaudium*, 35)

• • • • • • • • • • • • • • • • • • • • • • • • • • • • • • • •

Colleagues from these "non-traditional" areas are often involved in a variety of projects. For example, a working relationship with the campus grounds foreman could lead to a plan for the creation of a labyrinth on campus. Regular communication with institutional advancement staff could result in a workshop to help staff to better understand and tell the institution's story to potential donors. The director of a satellite campus may have a great idea for developing resources about the history and mission of the college for display at the site, but isn't sure how to obtain the necessary resources. A faculty member leading a study abroad program could incorporate religious art of a visiting country into the course syllabus. A working relationship with people from these areas may result in a bevy of projects for promoting and advancing the mission in non-traditional places.

## Funding

Funding for religious art and related projects is crucial. Many mission officers look in their own budgets only to realize that funding simply isn't there. This is where relationships and creativity come into play. Before meeting with key stakeholders, the type of art pieces wanted must be determined. Consider asking the president to contribute to the purchase of several small pieces. Many presidents have "special project funds" set aside for purposes such as this and are happy to contribute. Additionally, donors and alumni are often looking for small ways in which to contribute to the college in support of the mission. A conversation with the chief advancement officer could result in the surfacing of some opportunities. A senior class gift is another option. The mission officer might suggest a piece of religious art that the class consider underwriting. A retiring faculty member may be interested in donating a personal artifact to the school. Finally, board members who have a particular interest in the fine arts could be another option. Regardless, having a good working relationship with the college's advancement staff is essential.

## Structures

Mission officers can't "go it alone." Structures must be in place that support, advise, and guide the mission officer in his or her efforts to advance the mission of the college. Such structures can be a venue for discussing new ideas and strategies and eliciting support from other members of the campus community. Mission councils are a wonderful resource. These groups can include representatives who have a stake in mission integration and planning efforts. Their participation helps the mission officer build a coalition of supporters who can partner on projects. Subcommittees focused on specific projects such as religious art and symbolism can be helpful, especially if art professors, theology faculty, and interested students are involved. Mission officers don't have to be experts in everything, but they should be able to bring people together, facilitate projects and proposals, and know where to find resources.

By including the Vice President for Mission as a member of the Lewis University campus master plan committee, the institutional Catholic story was able to be visibly conveyed through art, symbolism, and architecture. This also shapes guiding principles for all future campus master planning initiatives.

Mission officers also have the responsibility to advocate for the advancement of mission as part of major campus structures. Many mission officers hold cabinet-level positions. They have access to other decision makers who can help advance certain kinds of projects or build support for them. Mission officers are often involved in strategic planning and campus master planning committees as well. Involvement on these committees is an opportunity to ensure that initiatives and efforts related to art, symbolism, and telling the institutional story are included.

The mission officer who has substantive relationships with an extensive group of campus constituencies, funding strategies, structures for input from diverse individuals, and implementation methods can best advance the institutional Catholic story through art, symbolism, and campus architecture. More importantly, displaying beautiful works of art connects students, faculty, and staff with opportunities to deepen their understanding of the rich heritage of the institution's charism, and come to a better understanding of the university's Catholic tradition.

*Kurt Schackmuth is Vice President for Mission and Academic Services at Lewis University, Romeoville, IL.*

## chapter Six
● ● ● ● ● ●

### Cardinal Newman: An Intriguing Voice for Mission Officers

*Edward Jeremy Miller*

Cardinal Newman is an intriguing champion not only for mission but for all aspects of Catholic higher education. His book, *Idea of a University*, is the classic defense of liberal arts-grounded undergraduate education; yet, he was accused by some intellectuals of his day, such as Principal A. M. Fairbairn, of promoting skepticism. Pope Leo XIII honored him with a cardinal's hat in 1878, yet under the previous pope, Pius IX, many in the Curia thought him heretical. "From first to last education...has been my line," he noted in his diary (*Autobiographical Writings*, 259), yet the Catholic archbishop of Westminster, Henry Edward Manning, blocked him from going to Oxford University to serve young Catholic undergraduates, ironically involving the very type of ministry that now goes by the Church-encouraged title of "Newman Clubs." These curiosities are but a few about Newman the educator, writer, and Catholic priest.

Today Newman is roundly lauded both by the Catholic Church and the Anglican Church, to which he belonged until 1845 when he became a Roman Catholic. Rome saw fit to beatify him when Pope Benedict XVI declared him to be Blessed John Henry on September 19, 2010, in Newman's adopted city of Birmingham. His feast day is designated as October 9, the date of his conversion. A champion of Catholic higher education, he forever remains: for his defense of it, his cautions about its potential fault lines, and his strategies for its advancement.

Newman is as instructive today as his career was intriguing then. Four areas will be considered here: hiring appropriate personnel, universities as places for exploring ideas rather than mandating dogma, student formation in Catholicism to advance the common good, and student formation of conscience. Before turning to them, a caution needs to be sounded. Newman wrote with subtlety and nuance because he chose to write about complex and delicate Catholic matters. Some quote him selectively and thereby misrepresent his thought. Very conservative Catholics see him as the champion of rigid authority. Very liberal Catholics quote him to support dissent from authority. His thoughts defy these narrow categories. When his balanced approach to complexities is rightly grasped, it is understandable why Benedict XVI, and John Paul II before him, gave Newman unreserved papal approval. Here's an illustration of the needed caution in quoting Newman. In an 1868 letter, Newman wrote, "It is *essential* that the Church should have a living presence and control in the action of the University." But the sentence that follows says, "But still, till the Bishops leave the University to itself, till the University governs itself, till it is able to act as a free being, it will be but a sickly child" (Newman, *Letters and Diaries*, Newman to Bartholomew Woodlock, March 4, 1868, 24:46). To quote either sentence selectively misrepresents Newman's thought; together they capture his nuanced insight into Catholic higher education governance.

## Hiring the Right Personnel

The foremost piece of advice Newman would pass to mission officers is the importance of hiring the right personnel, whether within the faculty, the staff, or the administration. It was captured by his notion of personal influence. "An academic system without personal influence of teachers [or others] upon pupils, is an arctic winter; it will create an ice-bound, petrified, cast-iron University, and nothing else" (*Historical Sketches* III, UE, 74). This advice extends beyond the needed expertise to do the job, such as counseling skills in residence life, savviness in marketing, and subject expertise in academics. For the Irish Catholic University to work, Newman, its first rector, was most circumspect about the proctors he appointed to supervise the three residence halls and the professors he hired to teach. He sought personnel who integrated in their personal lives Catholic values and the needed skills. Here is a morsel of his very first sermon from the brand-new university church on Stephen's Green, delivered to assembled faculty, staff, and students:

"Deductions have no power of persuasion. The heart is commonly reached, not through the reason, but through the imagination, by means of direct impressions, by the testimony of facts and events, by history, by description. Persons influence us, voices melt us, looks subdue us, deeds inflame us. Many a man will live and die upon a dogma: no man will be a martyr for a conclusion." (*Grammar of Assent,* UE, 93)

> [Academics and religion] should be found in one and the same place, and exemplified in the same persons. I want to destroy that diversity of centres…. I wish the same spots and the same individuals to be at once oracles of [academics] and shrines of devotion…. It will not satisfy me if religion is here and [academics] there…. I want the same roof to contain both the intellectual and moral discipline. (*Sermons Preached on Various Occasions*, UE, 13)

He feared separating academic and character formation. Our students, he would advise, are more influenced by integrated individuals working in the university than by clever programs or cleverer curriculum sheets. In Newman's mind, hiring for mission is critically important.

## Teaching and Exploring Ideas, Not Indoctrination

His second piece of advice is a reminder that colleges are places where ideas are explored, sifted, and critiqued but not indoctrinated. This seems obvious, almost banal, and to secular universities it would be. For mission officers of a Catholic college or university, it remains healthy advice, lest a Catholic college copy the pedagogy of seminary teaching. He began *Idea of a University* with the arresting phrase, "a University…is a place of *teaching* universal *knowledge*" (ix, italics his). He avoided intentionally saying "teaching truths."

Truthful insights should emerge from a process, and the word *knowledge* better fits the process. Here are a few implications. "It is the very law of the human mind in its inquiry…to make its advances by a process which…is circuitous. There are no shortcuts to knowledge…. In scientific researches error may be said, without paradox, to be in some instances the way to truth, and the only way" (*Ibid.*, 474). Newman trusted in the upshot of healthy debate. "[We] should be content to wait, knowing that error is

[A university] is a place to which a thousand schools make contribution; in which the intellect may safely range and speculate, sure to find its equal in some antagonist activity, and its judge in the tribunal of truth. It is a place where inquiry is pushed forward, and rashness rendered innocuous, and error exposed, by the collision of mind with mind, and knowledge with knowledge." (*Historical Sketches III*, 16)

like other delinquents; give it rope enough, and it will be found to have a strong suicidal propensity" (*Ibid.*, 467). Therefore, *process* rather than *control* should be the vocabulary tools of mission officers.

## Student Formation in a Catholic Worldview to Advance the Common Good

Who benefits from the mission of a Catholic college? All students should benefit, of course. But Newman had in mind Catholic undergraduates, unlike campuses today with students of every religious background or none at all. In all his pieces of advice, his parochial focus must be remembered. He wanted his graduates to enter into the national life of Ireland and England, shaping their laws, their public opinion, their industries and media. And he wanted them to witness to their Catholicism in an intelligent and persuasive manner. Let this then serve as his third piece of advice: focus on what students, surely Catholic students, are to become as transformative agents in the world.

> You [graduates should] be able to dispense on all sides of you the royal light of Truth, and exert an august moral influence upon the world…. It is a moral force, not a material, which will vindicate your profession, and will secure your triumph. It is not giants who do the most…. I want an intelligent, well-instructed laity….I wish you to enlarge your knowledge, to cultivate your reason, to get an insight into the relation of truth to truth….In all times the laity have been the measure of the Catholic spirit. (*Present Position of Catholics*, UE, 389-90)

Catholic higher education, in Newman's mind, has a significant responsibility to graduate individuals dedicated to advancing the common good through the lenses of a Catholic worldview. The mission officer can play a strategic role in ensuring that outcome.

## The Formation of Student Conscience

The last piece of advice from him—something at the core of all his spiritual writings—would be to foster formation of conscience. This should seem natural to mission officers, concerned as they are with promoting an institution's faithfulness to its founding spirit. Think of the latter as the institution's conscience, the voice of its soul, just as Newman calls a person's conscience the voice of "One to whom we are responsible" (*Grammar of Assent*, UE, 109). So it stands to reason that Newman would want to know how a Catholic

"We need to distinguish clearly what might be a fruit of the Kingdom from what runs counter to God's plan. This involves not only recognizing and discerning spirits, but also—and this is decisive—choosing movements of the spirit of good and rejecting those of the spirit of evil." (*Evangelii Gaudium*, 51)

● ● ● ● ● ● ● ● ● ● ● ● ● ● ● ● ● ● ● ● ● ● ● ● ● ● ● ● ● ● ● ●

university is assisting students with their conscience formation. An upper level morals or ethics class is a start, but is it enough? Spiritual direction, retreats, and sacramental confession are all good, but how many students are engaged in these activities? Participating in service-learning classes where reflection papers are required is helpful, but how many students seek out these classes? Judicial processes can be teaching moments if student affairs staff members are trained in a reconciliatory judicial process, but how often do they use the routine protocols of infractions and punishments? If the university's mission is concerned with the mind and soul, with the body and spirit of undergraduates, then conscience formation is essential. Conscience is to the soul as concepts are to the mind. It's for mission officers, as it was for Newman, to advance the interplay of both. In Newman's words:

> If I looked into a mirror, and did not see my face, I should have the sort of feeling which actually comes upon me, when I look into this busy living world, and see no reflection of its Creator.... Were it not for this voice, speaking so clearly in my conscience and my heart, I should be an atheist, or a pantheist. (Newman, *Apologia Pro Vita Sua*, UE, 241)

## Conclusion

In the person of John Henry Cardinal Newman, Catholic higher education has a dedicated and versed educator of the highest order whom the Church has recognized for his commitment to Catholic higher education and the Catholic faith. Mission officers would do well to read his many writings and apply them to today's Catholic university, so as to strengthen society, the Church, and higher education.

*NB: The Uniform Edition (UE) reproduces Newman's final edits and the very format he wished for his books. All pagination remained consistent as long as the UE was reprinted, which it is not now. However, the entire UE can be accessed at www.newmanreader.org.*

*Edward Jeremy Miller is Professor, Department of Religious Studies at Gwynedd Mercy University, Gwynedd Valley, PA.*

*References*

Newman, J. (1912). *Idea of a University*, Uniform Edition. London: Longmans.

Newman, J. (1957). *Autobiographical Writings*, New York: Sheed & Ward.

Newman, J. (1962). *Letters and Diaries of John Henry Newman*, London and Oxford.

## chapter SEVEN

## Aligning Brand and Mission: The Mission Officer's Role

*Margaret Kelly*

Brand is an important tool to help realize mission. "Brand" originated with use of hot metal pokers with symbols that burned through an animal's hair to leave a scar on the hide forever indicating the ranch/owner. But branding a college or university is not as simple as branding cattle for mere identification. Branding in alignment with mission has the power to focus an institution's operations and impact. If done right, branding can help to bring in more students, attract outstanding faculty, augment grants, and improve institutional efficiency and effectiveness. The mission officer must understand brand and how it works in order to serve as a steward and advocate in the process required for brand to become an organic reality. It is the rare institution that has identified the mission officer as having this role, but the benefits of doing so can be significant.

A successful brand is a signature or handle that opens to one's mission. Brand can be the entry point to explore, fall in love with, and experience mission. An effective brand distinguishes an institution, its programs, employees, students, and graduates. Brand is the institutional imprint, what one is known for or known to be. Ideally, one wants to be and be known for the same thing. A poor brand is like a half-open door missing its doorknob.

Every institution has a brand, whether it is intentional or not. People who don't know the institution form opinions based on information they acquire from a variety of sources—including Facebook and other social media. If an institution's brand is unclear, the chances of attracting desirable students and other resources are diminished. Branding is a powerful means of influencing perception.

Brand is visible in logos, tag lines, advertisements, websites, speeches, publications, policies, and every version of messaging. The mission officer's participation early in the process of determining brand is critical. Once a brand is chosen, it is a garment worn for many seasons. Its "accessories"—the tag lines and campaigns—will change with different audiences and initiatives. The greatest impact on the power and sustainability of brand is people. From the president to the telephone operator to the maintenance staff, it is the people who are the message. A mission officer's role in relation to brand is to help the institution generate and project the most appropriate messages, and live them. They should derive from the mission and should lead, guide, and resonate within people.

Missions are message. Brands are message. One could argue, theoretically, that mission and brand are one. Jesus is the best example of mission and brand integration. Jesus is Word, Logos. He is what he taught: love, surrender. He lived (lives) in the posture of "yes." But, for most of us, that "oneness" is a work in progress.

Branding to support mission is all about "Word" in the holiest of interpretations. Institutions are called to live their brands, just as they are called to live their missions. If the community is living its mission,

"Jesus is 'the first and greatest evangelizer'... [and God] has called us to cooperate with him." (*Evangelii Gaudium*, 12)

and its brand is aligned with its mission, good happens. When the brand does not reflect mission, there is trouble. The mission officer is responsible for delivering that insight and sustaining the institutional dialog that addresses it.

Those responsible for the institution's messaging must be aware of mission implications. For example, if the institution's mission affirms the dignity of the human person and the oneness of the human family, and its brand expresses a commitment to the global community, yet it advertises on a radio talk show that consistently demeans an ethnic group or denies responsibility for immigrants, is this not a serious disconnect? If the mission officer does not question these things, who will? Courage will be needed to advance Catholic identity.

Brands should be mission-driven. Any initiative to rebrand an institution should begin with questions. "Who are we and what is our purpose?" "How are we perceived?" "For what do we want to be known?" "What makes us stand apart from the crowd?" "What should our brand promise be to students?" The mission officer needs to be in on this conversation.

"...[T]oday's vast and rapid cultural changes demand that we constantly seek ways of expressing unchanging truths in a language which brings out their abiding newness." (*Evangelii Gaudium*, 41)

Rebranding is akin to publishing a new translation of the Bible. The Truth does not change, but the articulation does; meaning is clarified; emphases and nuances are revealed. When an outside vendor is brought in to facilitate rebranding, it is important that the vendor partners with the "experts" who know their institution best. The president must make it clear to everyone, including trustees and marketing administrators, that it is appropriate for the mission officer to serve on the steering committee and to participate in the dialogue of planning and selecting the vendor.

The mission officer together with the president must guard the integrity of the institution. The call is to communicate the truth of what the institution is in a way that persuades others to participate in its life. One way this can be done is to use Catholic language in messaging without waving the flag of religion as religion. Catholic identity needs to permeate the learning environment. The institution should communicate what students will experience in their education that aligns with founding principles and with the charism that makes the institution relevant in the world today.

For example, why not use the word *vocation* and connect it to "careers that serve?" This language connotes financial success and personal advancement, as well as a sense of responsibility to give back to others. Prospective students who desire to help others want to know that the institution they choose is one that shares their goals.

To reflect Catholic language more directly one might substitute: "God-given potential" for "potential," "service for the common good" for "community service," "moral and ethical" for "ethical," and "social justice" for "justice." Space limitations for banners and headlines may preclude Catholic language, but descriptions and elaborations can support Catholic Tradition.

The role of the mission officer is crucial in determining the framework or brand that promises outcomes to students. Both the mission officer and the marketing administrator need to realize that: The meaning of a holistic education is different today than it was pre-Internet; literacy has a much broader meaning today; ethics must include e-mail ethics; and global awareness has amplified the understanding of family and community.

Working with the administrator responsible for marketing is essential. The bond of collegial friendship aimed at shared values between the mission officer and the administrator for marketing needs to be cultivated and nourished. The mission officer should not interfere in the daily details of tactical marketing, but it is advisable to maintain a watchful eye and to question what may drift off-brand. The mission officer does not assume the posture of the "brand police." That is the responsibility of marketing. Assisting the marketing staff and acknowledging their good work will strengthen this vital relationship.

The mission officer seeks to advance the founding vision and celebrate excellence. Alert to politics, he or she is an idealist and realist who knows the importance of timing. The effective mission officer aligns with those in authority and creates credibility. It is important to identify concordance as well as discrepancies between brand and mission. The mission officer is the champion of institutional change, but allows others to be the heroes. First-rate mission orientation programs followed by collaborative continuing education programs on mission will reap significant benefits.

The mission officer needs to have strong working relationships and regular communication both with those handling the messaging and with the president. Creating a climate where all questions are welcome in the spirit of collaboration makes the mission officer a powerful catalyst for correction and celebration.

Catholic colleges and universities have similar missions because they derive their purpose from the same source, Jesus and Gospel values based on His life. Institutional brands should be in accord with those same values. As missions emphasize different reflections of those values, brands also will present different configurations of emphasis and manifestation.

All strive for missions that are consistent in manifesting Catholicity. All want to have and live brands that enhance their missions, as well as market who they are and what they have to offer. They want to provide options for others to choose them as partners on their journeys of vocation, spirituality, and finding meaning and fulfillment. As a champion of the institution's brand, the mission officer acts as an advocate to encourage, strengthen, and advance the university's mission. In this way, students' lives are transformed. The result is that the college or university, its faculty, staff, students, and alumni help to manifest "Thy Kingdom come, Thy Will be done."

*Margaret Kelly is Vice President for Mission at Holy Family University, Philadelphia, PA.*

# chapter EIGHT

●●●●●●

## Writing a Catholic Identity Statement: From Prickly to Purposeful

### *Gertrude Rompré*

A Catholic Identity Statement (CIS) is a written statement detailing a collective understanding of an institution's Catholic identity, including both the values on which it is based and how it is lived out in its day-to-day operations. As such, the process of creating a CIS can reinvigorate a college or university community. It refocuses the community on its core identity from which it can draw life. Nevertheless, the process can also uncover some "prickly" questions, which will need to be addressed before the deeper purpose of the CIS can be actualized. The question then is: How can we transform the process of writing a Catholic Identity Statement from prickly to purposeful?

A cursory search of the websites of Catholic colleges and universities in the United States will reveal that a significant number have taken on the task of creating a CIS. Usually housed in the "about" section of a website under "mission and identity," a CIS can range from a "one-liner" to full-blown discussion papers reflecting on an institution's charism, history, and ongoing values. What these have in common, however, is that they reveal their institution's explicit desire to name who they are and from where their mission is derived.

There is an intimate connection between Catholic identity and mission. While not one and the same, the two concepts live in relationship. Mission flows out of, and is shaped by, an institution's Catholic identity. In turn, Catholic identity is strengthened as its mission is lived out in concrete ways. A mission well-lived will speak volumes about an institution's identity. However, this is often not enough. The idea that students, faculty, and staff will "get" what it means to be a Catholic college or university simply by osmosis, by bathing in the collective pool of Catholic thought and commitment,

> "Every Catholic University is to make known its Catholic identity, either in a mission statement or in some other appropriate public document...." (*Ex corde Ecclesiae*, Part 2, 2.3)

●●●●●●●●●●●●●●●●●●●●●●●●●●●●●●●●●●●●

can no longer be taken for granted. Catholic identity needs to be articulated and named to be effectively passed on.

Before this process occurs, however, those prickly questions that often surround the creation of a Catholic Identity Statement need to be addressed:

*Is there one Catholic identity?* There are as many incarnations of Catholic identity as there are Catholics. How, then, can an academic institution write a statement of Catholic identity? The key, here, is to differentiate between individual and collective identity. What the CIS is meant to do is to describe a corporate sense of "self" that flows out of its institution's Catholic heritage and commitment. A CIS serves to name an institution's collective identity, allowing individuals to recognize themselves within that statement to varying degrees. At its best, the statement ought to call forth an ever-deepening commitment to the workings of the institution as it is Catholic.

*Can Catholic identity be inclusive?* How does creating a corporate statement of Catholic identity allow an institution to remain inclusive of those of other Christian denominations, other religious traditions, or those who espouse no faith? Perhaps it is useful, here, to turn the question on its head. Can an exclusive statement ever be catholic? If the word *catholic* is understood in its broadest sense, in terms of universality, it becomes clear that to be catholic, indeed, means to be inclusive. In practical terms, the CIS is an invitation to dialogue between all members of a university community and its faith tradition. Having an expressed sense of identity allows for more developed relationships among those with differing views, in that points of difference and points of convergence can more clearly be identified.

*Who gets to shape Catholic identity?* On a big-picture level, an institution's Catholic identity emerges as interplay between its heritage, its connection with the wider Catholic Intellectual Tradition, and internal dialogue. In practice, however, intentional processes need to be put in place to create a venue or a forum for this type of interplay. The mandate to create a CIS can come from a variety of sources. The president or trustees may be first to identify the need. Perhaps it is a strategic planning initiative. In some cases, the mission officer may be the first to name the need for the CIS. Whatever the provenance of the task, the actual initiation of the process often falls to the mission officer. What practical considerations must be taken into account when creating such a process?

What follows might be titled, "Catholic Identity Statements in Five Easy (or not so easy!) Steps" or the "5 C's of Catholic Identity Statements." On a less flippant note, however, it would seem that five elements are required for the successful creation of a statement that reflects to a fair degree the Catholic identity of a college or university.

## Step One: Choose

In collaboration with the president, choose wisely the members of a working group or task force charged with the creation of a CIS. These individuals will make or break (brake) the process. This group will need to represent as wide a segment of the institution as possible. It should represent a balance of voices including students, staff, and faculty, women and men, Catholics and non-Catholics, trustees and members of the sponsoring congregation (if applicable), newcomers and folks with institutional memory. It is important that those chosen to serve on this committee be dedicated to the ongoing vitality of the institution's Catholic identity and have expertise such as writing skills, theological knowledge, and charism wisdom. At the same time, they must be open to the delicate negotiation that will be part of creating a statement that speaks to a much broader constituency. It becomes the task of this group to decide on the format of the statement (if not predetermined by other administrative bodies) and to write its first draft.

## Step Two: Create

In deciding on the format of the final document—anything ranging from the one-liner to the full-blown working paper—it is necessary to clarify the primary purposes of the statement. Is it a simple phrase to be put on websites and promotional materials to capture the imagination? Is it a formation tool? Is it to be used as a basis for making policy? To whom will it be addressed? Will it target a narrow audience, or is it meant for public consumption, including those outside the university or college community? Discussion of this sort is a necessary precursor to the actual creation of a draft document. It is also wise to keep the president, trustees, and sponsoring bodies apprised of decisions made every step of the way.

A second tool that can be used is a table to help brainstorm the key pillars of Catholic identity as it is currently lived out in the institution (see appendix). A helpful presumption to make is that its Catholic identity is alive and well. If that is not entirely the case, perhaps the committee will have to seek out those dusty corners where it resides and coax it out! Either way, the table format allows the committee to name the moment in terms of Catholic identity and to use this as a starting point. Once this exercise is complete, the committee will review to see if there are any major gaps in its synopsis of the lived Catholic identity of the institution. If so, these missing pieces can be added. If not, a member (or two) of the committee can be charged with writing the first draft, which will then be vetted by the entire committee.

## Step Three: Collaborate/Consult

Once the first draft of the Catholic Identity Statement is completed, it is time to take the show on the road. Consult, consult, consult! First, bring the draft to those who have mandated its creation, then expand the consultation. Casting a wide net for feedback will make up for the inherent limitations of a small working group and, in the long run, create an atmosphere most conducive to eventual buy-in on the part of the entire community. Focus groups can be created, allowing various constituencies to comment on the document. At this stage, it is important that everyone from food services to administration have a chance to be heard. Specific questions can be asked:

- What stands out for you in the CIS?
- What is puzzling or difficult to understand?
- In what ways do you most recognize your work in the CIS?
- What would you like to see added or changed?
- What do you like about the CIS?
- Does the CIS reflect us?
- How well does the CIS address its stated purposes?
- How effective is the review process?

The draft ought to be presented to various bodies within the institution depending on its organizational structure.

## Step Four: Change

Step four almost goes without saying. Once feedback is collected, be willing to change the draft accordingly. Of course, this process will require wisdom, as some of the feedback will most likely be contradictory. On the other hand, recognition that the broader voices have been heard will, again, bode well for the eventual acceptance of the statement by the university community as a whole.

## Step Five: Communicate

Finally, it comes time to communicate the statement to the world. This comes in two forms, the formal and the informal. Undoubtedly, the statement will require approvals and ratification by various levels of governance ensuring that it, indeed, represents the collective will of the institution. Presentations will have to be made to cabinets, boards of trustees, faculty councils, and so forth. Motions will have to be proposed and passed, giving the statement the heft it needs to speak on behalf of the college or university.

Once approved, the document will have to be distributed widely and integrated into websites and other promotional materials. It may be used as a benchmark document to reflect on current programs and initiatives. It may, also, be used to inspire deeper thought about the vision and mission of the whole. The mission belongs to everyone, and the extent to which it is lived out depends on each individual's understanding and willingness to commit to it. The CIS, then, becomes a tool to foster this commitment. In doing so, it may even bring new life to the institution.

At its core, the creation of a Catholic Identity Statement is a work of the Holy Spirit. Done right, the process itself can unleash a creative energy, allowing people to name their passion for Catholic Higher Education and to renew their commitment to it. Dealing with the prickly questions at the front end of the process will best prepare the community to allow the breath of the Spirit—*ru'ach*—to breeze through and bring life. After all, Catholic identity is incarnated in the people who live and breathe it. The Catholic Identity Statement, then, simply serves to celebrate their vocation.

*Gertrude Rompré is Director of Mission and Ministry at St. Thomas More College, University of Saskatchewan, Canada.*

| Appendix: Concise Inventory of Catholic Identity, Heritage, and Practice | | | | | | | |
|---|---|---|---|---|---|---|---|
| | Theme 1: Catholic Intellectual Tradition | Theme 2: Catholic Social Teaching | Theme 3: Catholic Prayer and Worship | Theme 4: The Catholic Aesthetic | Theme 5: Inclusivity | Theme 6: | Theme 7: |
| Content | | | | | | | |
| How do we live this out at _____? | | | | | | | |
| Reflection questions | | | | | | | |
| Illustrations | | | | | | | |
| Conclusion: Invitation to dialogue and continued conversation | | | | | | | |

## section TWO
● ● ● ● ● ●

**The Roles, Responsibilities, and Skills of the Mission Officer**

## chapter NINE

## Professionalization of the Mission Leader

*Michael J. James*
*Joseph J. Lehman, TOR*
*Oscar Mayorga*

A process of professionalization for mission leaders in Catholic higher education should be strategically advanced. This chapter will propose common characteristics of an effective mission leader through an examination of the findings from recent research about the mission leader in Catholic higher education[1], as well as the related but distinct history of leaders of mission services in Catholic health care.

Professionalization is the social process that tends to involve establishing acceptable qualifications, an agreed upon canon of knowledge, a professional body or association to oversee the conduct of members of the profession, and some degree of demarcation between levels of demonstrated competence. Although the appointment of a mission leader in Catholic higher education is a recent phenomenon, mission leaders have rapidly become a reality on a majority of Catholic colleges and universities in the United States. However, mission leaders have yet to establish norms, competencies, and codes of conduct articulated by and handed on through professional development strategies enforced by a body of peers.

During the 1970s, a decade before the first mission leader was established at a Catholic college or university, Catholic health care began the process of assigning women religious as leaders of mission services to keep the connection between the Church and the ministry alive. For Catholic health care, the mission leader's role, work requirements, and salary often varied from hospital to hospital. There were few opportunities for professional training, such as internships or mentoring. Consequently, the early mission leader in Catholic health care usually had to both define and legitimize her position in the organization (Grant, *Health Progress*, 1999).

According to the research about Catholic health care conducted by Dr. Kathryn Grant, a mission leader's responsibilities were often unclear, and as a result, some mission leaders lacked legitimacy in their organizations. Although mission leaders, as Grant describes, led prayers, organized retreats, and coordinated charity drives, they were rarely able to influence their organization's decision-making processes. Some were actually denied access to those processes.

---

1  *Data on the mission leader in Catholic higher education is based on research conducted by and presented at the ACCU Annual Meetings in 2011 and 2012 by Michael James, Oscar Mayorga, and Joseph Lehman, OSF, as well as a dissertation in process by Joseph Lehman, a doctoral candidate in the Higher Education program at Boston College.*

In Catholic higher education, mission leaders oversee an increasingly complex organizational structure, but admittedly without the life-and-death consequences or the complex ethical challenges that occasionally face the mission leader within the Catholic health care system. However, the potentially significant influence of a mission leader to contribute to institutional mission-capacity-building in Catholic higher education should not be underestimated.

The Office of Mission and Ministry on a Catholic university or college campus is usually established under the leadership of, reports directly to, and advises the president. The mission leader typically serves on the following university committees: President's Council, Institutional Catholic Identity Committee, Board of Trustees Mission Committee, Institutional Strategic Planning Committee, and Senior Academic Officer's Committee. The typical Mission Unit (often to include the coordination of the Office of Campus Ministry as well as a variety of other discrete student development programs and institutes of study related to the sponsoring religious community's charism) employs: 3.4 full-time professional staff; 1.3 part-time professional staff; 1.3 full-time support staff; 1 part-time support staff; 1 graduate student assistant; and 5 undergraduate students. The average annual operating budget (excluding salaries/benefits) is <$50,000. The unit is supported solely by institutional funds without supplemental grants or endowment income.

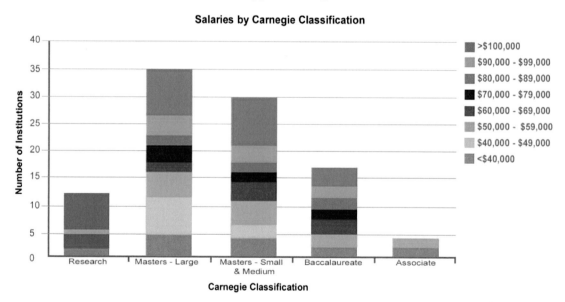

A typical Mission Unit at a Catholic college or university coordinates, or is significantly engaged in the hiring and selection process for administrators and orientation programs for faculty, administrators, and staff. The Mission Unit is moderately involved in continuing formation programs for administrators, staff, faculty, trustees, and students. The Mission Unit is not engaged in the faculty tenure and review process or annual performance review process for administrators and staff. The Mission Unit participates in some form of assessment of the effectiveness of mission integration on campus.

Research on mission leaders in Catholic higher education reveals an interesting pattern in their perceptions about the degree of impact that the mission unit has on the roles and responsibilities of each campus constituent group both internal and external to the campus. By contrast, internal constituents (e.g., administrators, faculty, and students) are perceived by mission leaders to experience a higher degree of impact by mission unit activities overall than external constituent groups (e.g., alumni and diocese). This finding is of no surprise. However, a comparison of impact within internal constituent groups reveals the perception that students and faculty (arguably the key internal constituent groups) experience the lowest degree of impact. This latter finding should sensitize mission leaders to pay close attention to the actual outcomes of impact on students and faculty through their own rigorous assessment processes.

**Mission Leaders' Perceptions of the Impact of the Mission Unit on Institutional Constituencies**

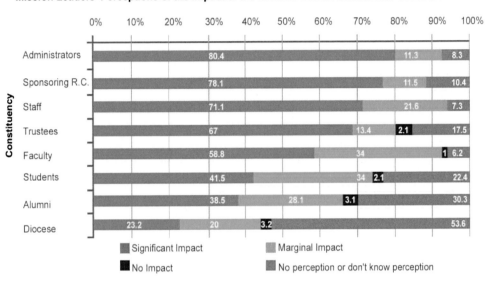

A relationship exists between the Mission Unit's involvement in orientation and ongoing education programs and the perceived impact on faculty members' roles and responsibilities. For example, Mission Units that either "coordinate" or are "significantly involved" in both orientation *and* ongoing mission formation of faculty are more than twice as likely to believe the Mission Unit is making a "significant impact" versus a "marginal impact" upon faculty members' work. On the other hand, Mission Units that are "moderately," "minimally," or "not engaged" in orientation and ongoing mission formation of faculty are five times more likely to believe the Mission Unit is making a "marginal impact" versus a "significant impact" upon faculty members' work.

At Molloy College, the following ongoing mission initiatives by the Dominican college have been transformative:
- Annual Summer Study Program for students, faculty, staff in Fanjeaux, France.
- Biennial Dominican Colleges' Colloquium – academic focus.
- Call for Papers incorporates the Four Pillars of Dominican Life.
- Revised Mission Statement (2008), which articulates the Four Pillars.
- Visits to Dominican Motherhouse for History/Heritage.
- Dominican Young Adults – chapter on campus.
- Service in Dominican-sponsored ministries locally, nationally, and internationally.

**Mission Leaders' Perceptions of Impact Upon Faculty through Orientation & Ongoing Education Programs**

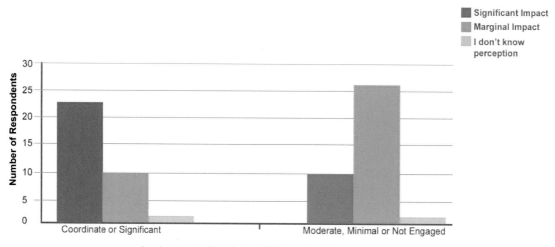

Involvement In Orientation AND Ongoing Education

Since the mid-1980s Catholic health care has been working to identify the competencies required in a professional mission leader. Although a common core of broad-based competencies has been difficult to solidify due to the distinct cultures that operate across institutions, Grant reports a general concurrence that a mission leader needs the pastoral qualities of compassion, approachability, and the ability to listen—combined with business and organizational savvy, as well as negotiation and persuasion skills. Within Catholic health care it is also agreed that although mission will vary across institutional cultures, the mission leader's main task is to ensure the integration of mission imperatives into the organization's strategic planning and vision for the future.

Where do mission leaders in Catholic higher education stand on the matter of qualifications and competencies? According to the 2010 survey results of mission leaders in Catholic higher education, it is generally agreed that the following characteristics, divided into three discreet categories, are highly desirable for an effective mission leader:

Professional Qualifications and Experience
• Academic credibility
• Terminal degree in an academic discipline
• Faculty teaching and scholarship
• Educational administrative experience
• Seniority and knowledge of the institution
• Formative experience within the sponsor's charis

Personal Qualities and Attributes
• Personable                    • Persistent
• Passionate                    • Prayerful
• Imaginative                   • Self-motivated
• Honest
• Flexible
• Open
• Patient

Competencies (knowledge, skills, and abilities)
- Knowledge of
  - o  Sponsoring charism and heritage
  - o  Theology
  - o  Catholic Social Thought
  - o  Catholic Intellectual Tradition
  - o  Institutional history and internal culture
  - o  Current issues in Catholic higher education
- Skills in
  - o  Communication
  - o  Collaboration
  - o  Relationship-building
  - o  Organizational management
- Ability to
  - o  Articulate institutional mission & values
  - o  Negotiate a diverse campus culture
  - o  Think creatively about mission strategies

What is called for is a robust and intentional process of professionalization of the mission leader in Catholic higher education informed by the above attributes and qualifications. However, the successful implementation of a process for professionalization will depend upon several critical factors: cooperation with national association leadership; continued sharing of best practices among mission leaders; continued research, shared knowledge, and reflection on contemporary Catholic higher education; and the regular formative-assessment of constructive and evidence-based professional practices. An intentional and ongoing training process will be most effective if it is forward-thinking and collaboratively conceived across Catholic colleges and universities, with the intention of supporting the good work of current mission leaders, as well as attracting and preparing the next generation of aspiring mission leaders in Catholic higher education. With vision from within the community of mission leaders, these professional development programs could also serve as a coherent area of study that results in granting participants some form of credential or certification that would be recognized as a significant and even necessary achievement by an organizing body of peers and institutional leaders.

Current Formation Programs:
- The annual seminar for mission leaders at ACCU Annual Meetings.
- The Boston College Institute for Administrators in Catholic Higher Education.
- Participation in programs supported by institutions' sponsoring religious communities with a focus on distinct charisms.

Recommended Formation Programs:
- Senior mission leader mentoring of junior mission leaders.
- A semi-annual newsletter complemented by a repository of resources, programs, events, etc., accessible online.
- A national body of peers to codify standards of professional competency and effective practices.

*Michael J. James is Lecturer, Department of Educational Leadership & Higher Education, and Director of the Institute for Administrators in Catholic Higher Education, Boston College, Boston, MA.*

*Rev. Joseph J. Lehman, TOR is Director of Mission Integration at Saint Francis University, Loretto, PA.*

*Oscar J. Mayorga is a Research and Diversity Consultant, Boston, MA.*

---

*Reference*

Grant, M. K. "Catholic Healthcare Systems are Beginning to Develop Professional Mission Leaders" (pp. 18-21). *Health Progress*, 80, No. 2. March-April 1999.

## chapter TEN

## Pastoral, Educational, and Administrative: Finding Our Deepest Identity in Jesus

*Stephanie Russell*

Nearly twenty years after Pope John Paul II's apostolic constitution on Catholic universities, *Ex corde Ecclesiae*, and fifty years since the Second Vatican Council's call of all the baptized to a common priesthood, Catholic higher education is in the midst of animated and occasionally tense discussions about who is responsible for its fundamental mission and how that mission will be stewarded in the future. Among the outcomes of this ongoing conversation is the emergence of a new role on campus: the chief mission and identity officer. The construction and placement of the mission officer's role varies widely among Catholic educational institutions. Some are cabinet-level administrators; others are part-time appointees from the faculty. Often larger and more affluent universities staff complex and well-funded mission offices, while small colleges rely on the skills and creativity of a single coordinator. Many are ordained or vowed religious, though lay mission officers have begun to take their place in the ranks. Even the locus of accountability fluctuates from school to school. While most mission officers are hired and paid directly by their college or university, some are employees of the sponsoring religious community and are placed in the institution with the explicit charge of forging a connection between the school and the order.

"And what do you DO?" The personal banker I'd been assigned to was completing some paperwork for a car loan, filling in blanks and bubbles on a standardized form. "I'm a vice president for mission at a university." She studied me over her bejeweled glasses and, after a few moments, clucked out a bemused response. "Well! You don't see a lot of missionaries, these days, do you?"

Expectations for mission officers are as disparate as their institutions' histories, founding community charisms, and sensibilities surrounding the Church-university relationship. They are also reliant on the education, experience, and personalities of those who occupy the position. Using a theological lens may prove helpful for seeing "mission work" as the vocational and professional path it is rapidly becoming and how those who do the work organize it. If the university's mission is the mission of Christ, then how might mission work be understood in light of His life and ministry? The kingdom-building of Jesus, so evident in what the Church has come to identify as three principal offices—

those of priest, prophet, and king—provides guidance. It is helpful to remember that all Christians are called to find in themselves dimensions of these very identities and to exercise them on behalf of others. By framing the work in this manner, mission officers eschew anything that separates them from the campus community and get "back to basics" as servant leaders.

## Priest: The Pastoral Role

Most mission officers have experience in the pastoral care of others. They genuinely love faculty, staff, and students, and have enough faith in the future of their college or university to put their gifts to use on its behalf. Mission officers are called upon to lead or support the community in times of grief and loss, to pray in public settings, and to stay attuned to the spiritual barometer of the campus. In some cases, senior leaders rely on mission officers as partners in their work, or seek spiritual or retreat direction from them. In their counseling, preaching, writing, and community-building, mission officers must remain conscious of their role as bearers of the school's (and sometimes the order's) expression of Catholic tradition and the importance of staying in dialogue with campus ministers and other pastoral leaders. The officer's spiritual authenticity and maturity are paramount to his or her success, and help to avoid the cult of personality that can develop around high-profile pastoral lone rangers on a campus.

Ordained mission officers bring with them the advantage of being able to meet members of the community at particularly tender times in their lives—presiding at the Eucharist, or at the weddings and funerals of campus community members. On the other hand, the daily lives of lay mission officers are often more closely aligned to those of faculty and staff, and their ability to preach the Gospel in fresh and relevant ways gives them a distinctive credibility with others. Whether lay or ordained, pastoral duties can absorb the majority of the mission officer's time and attention at some schools. While few people would argue with the value of providing compassionate pastoral ministry on a Catholic campus, an exclusive focus on pastoral care effectively limits the amount of time available for addressing issues of formation, institutional integrity, or Catholic intellectual life. Balance among the offices of priest, prophet, and king is essential.

## Prophet: The Formational Role

To be a prophet is to convey the message of God's unyielding love. Prophets plant themselves deeply in the life of a community and bring the Word to bear on its experience. Rather than making themselves the focal point of faith, prophets call each person to respond authentically, according to his or her abilities, and trust that the love-message of God will be meaningful in the particularities of a person's life. For the mission officer, much of this work is done through the ministry of formation. Whether orienting new employees to the religious heritage of the institution or helping faculty learn to teach in its spiritual tradition, prophetic mission officers need to provide formational experiences that respond to the real-life concerns of faculty, staff, and students. Effective mission officers are deep listeners and keen observers of how universities work. They accompany others in exploring key questions at the heart of university life, such as:

- How can trustees and senior leaders (lay and ordained) be formed to see themselves as co-responsible for the mission of the institution?

- What curricular and co-curricular experiences can be created for students, in order to imprint upon them a deep commitment to faith and justice?
- What are the primary institutional markers of Catholic identity today, and what should they be in the future?
- How can non-Catholic Christians and non-Christians be invited into the Catholic mission of the university, while honoring their religious freedom?

Another understanding of the role of the prophet involves raising difficult issues related to moral and ethical choices. Mission officers will occasionally have uncomfortable conversations with other university leaders on inconsistencies between the university's stated mission and its everyday decisions. On rare occasions, the mission officer will voice a particularly unpopular point of view, emanating from his or her understanding of the university's mission. There is inherent personal risk in these moments for the mission officer who is not tenured and serves at the pleasure of the president. Jesus' admonition in Luke 9:24, "For whoever wishes to save his life will lose it, but whoever loses his life for my sake will save it," remains the standard of freedom toward which mission officers must strive. The temptation for those who are less spiritually grounded, however, is (1) to acquiesce in decisions that are contrary to the university's mission, or (2) to accept the mantle of being the "conscience of the university," a term utterly lacking in humility that does a disservice to the activity of the Holy Spirit in others. Mission officers are called to a continuous deepening of their spiritual lives, in order to discern the challenging choices that face them on a regular basis.

Perhaps the most powerful experiences of prophecy come when mission officers are confronted by students who perceive that the university is falling short of its stated purposes, and call it to live its mission more faithfully. While no one likes to be admonished, these moments of discord or discomfort ought to be celebrated as signs that the mission of Jesus has truly taken root in the student body. The mission officer can be a great encourager and humble teacher of these young prophets.

**King: The Administrative Role**

In addition to their pastoral and formational roles, many university mission officers spend significant time on administrative tasks: supervising staff, serving on the president's cabinet, consulting on policies and curricula, building and maintaining relationships with the local Church, and promoting mission-centered hiring practices. Some mission officers view their place at the decision-making table as *outwardly focused* (i.e., bringing information and perspective from the university leadership to the community), while others tend to be *inwardly focused* and speak of their responsibility for bringing concerns of the campus, local, national, or international community to bear on the leadership's deliberations. Both of these functions are important, and the self-reflective mission officer will be able to recognize his or her inclination toward one or the other.

The mission officer must remain vigilant, however, not to confuse the mere performance of executive tasks with the kingly identity of Jesus that all Christians are called to emulate. Jesus, who never occupied an administrative post, was not "kingly" by virtue of his job description or institutional portfolio. Rather, his authority and rule rested in service, sacrifice, and self-giving. Similarly, any resonance that a mission officer has with the kingship of Jesus will be found not in what he or she oversees in the institution, but in whether all tasks—administrative and otherwise—are undertaken with love.

The concept of kingship also connotes an ability to appreciate and actively engage the particularities of God's world. Catholic universities have a unique place in American higher education, but they also share many characteristics with their counterparts in the public and private spheres. Knowing the history and culture of American universities tends to advance mission work more quickly than operating as if one were deposited on the campus as a stranger in a strange land. Many missionaries of the Church spent years learning languages and studying new cultures before engaging in dialogue with local communities around meaningful questions of faith.

On a local level, the culture of any university is multi-layered. Familiarizing oneself with the institution's educational philosophy, processes for promotion and tenure, relationship with the sponsoring order, pedagogical tradition, leaders of the past, economic realities, and student body profile are all cues that the mission officer acknowledges that he or she is entering another culture. The mission officer must be prepared to recognize the activity of God, which began long before his or her arrival, in the incarnate life of the school.

The Vincentian Mission Institute (DePaul University, Niagara University, and St. John's University) offers senior leaders the opportunity to experience, learn about, and reflect on their institution's distinctive charism and Catholic identity. The two-year program includes online coursework, web conference discussions, capstone projects, and a heritage trip to France which leads to the integration of Catholic and Vincentian thinking into the participants' decision-making processes.

## Conclusion

In its earliest iterations, the work of mission officers had much to do with "mission awareness," familiarizing the faculty, staff, and students with the Catholic tradition and, in some situations, the specific spiritual charism of a sponsoring order. Both the role and its objectives have grown since those first forays into institutionalizing mission work. The work of mission officers is now more about the cultivation of mission leaders for the future—women and men, a core of Catholics and non-Catholics—who will commit themselves to embracing the mission of Catholic higher education and serve as priests, prophets, and kings to those around them. Catholic heritage must live in new ways, incorporating the gifts of lay, ordained, and religious mission leaders who together reflect the diversity of God's people.

*Stephanie Russell is Vice President for Mission and Ministry at Marquette University, Milwaukee, WI.*

## chapter ELEVEN

## Mission Officer as Catholic Cultural Catalyst, Convener, and Conscience

*Melanie Morey*

Mission officers at Catholic colleges and universities support and enrich their institution's Catholic culture and identity. While most mission officers operate with a small department and a limited budget, they make a big impact when they operate as *catalysts* and *conveners* who, in collaboration with fellow staff, students, faculty, trustees, and alumni, are the Catholic cultural *conscience* of their institutions.

### Catholic Cultural Catalyst

Catholic institutional culture is dynamic, not static. It is like a fire that will burn out unless constantly stoked. And who stokes these Catholic fires at Catholic colleges and universities? It is cultural catalysts, who do two very important things. First, they are role models who embody the best of Catholic culture, and by their very witness inspire others to embrace these ideals. Second, catalysts identify necessary cultural adaptations and changes, galvanizing the support of the community behind them with the aim of reinvigorating and reinforcing Catholic identity. A vibrant Catholic collegiate culture requires a number of catalysts at all levels, to be sure; and Catholic institutional identity and mission can be strengthened substantively when the mission officer is one of them.

"When certain categories of reason and the sciences are taken up into the proclamation of the message, these categories then become tools of evangelization; water is changed into wine." (*Evangelii Gaudium*, 132)

● ● ● ● ● ● ● ● ● ● ● ● ● ● ● ● ● ● ● ● ● ● ● ● ● ● ● ● ● ● ●

As a cultural catalyst, the mission officer is called to be a visible witness to the Catholic faith. He or she embodies the difference the faith makes in his or her own life as well as to the intellectual and social character of the institution. These individuals, along with others in the mission office, must exemplify and articulate that which is most compelling about the Catholic nature of Catholic higher education.

By engaging the community, faculty, and students, the mission officer has a programmatic role in determining what the institution needs to make its Catholic culture vital today, and into the future. In order to fulfill this programmatic role, the mission officer must gather information. A first step in gathering information is determining what is going on with respect to Catholic identity, mission, and character in all the various university divisions and departments. Ideally, the mission officer will attend religiously oriented activities sponsored by different units of the college or university and get to know the priorities and concerns of the community. Second, the mission officer needs hard data to determine whether these activities and programs are successful. For instance, senior exit surveys provide data that can be compared from year to year, both to note trends and to examine the effectiveness of particular programs. It is equally important to examine existing Catholic experiences, practices, and programs campus-wide both in terms of their impact and long-term viability. If programs have limited impact, or have lost their vitality or effectiveness, the mission officer would do well to have them replaced with more vibrant programs that make a difference. Finally, the mission officer should find out what is going on at comparable or competing Catholic institutions. If other institutions are effectively promoting their Catholic identity, some of their programs might flourish if adopted and/or adapted.

---

Mission-centric recruitment events at Mount St. Mary's involve the entire community. Administrators, faculty, staff, and students assist the Admissions Office in over seventy recruitment presentations each year. Speakers incorporate the university's mission and Catholic identity into presentations about their specific area of expertise, better equipping all staff members to talk about the mission and university as a whole.

· · · · · · · · · · · · · · · · · · · · · · · · · · · · · · ·

In catalyzing programmatic initiatives, the mission officer can also make a significant contribution by providing personnel and securing financing. Mission officers gain institutional clout when their offices go beyond encouraging good ideas and offer tangible implementation assistance. For example, they might establish a track record of obtaining access to grants from budget lines within the institution and take the initiative to seek external financing for new programs.

## Catholic Cultural Convener

A vibrant Catholic culture on campus blossoms when there is consistent integration of the Catholic intellectual and moral tradition across all departments and collegiate divisions. Every Catholic campus has faculty, administrators, and staff members who are knowledgeable about the tradition and committed to its integration. All too often, however, these individuals operate discretely and almost anonymously within their own spheres. As a result, students experience a series of intermittent Catholic moments rather than a vibrant Catholic culture that shapes their way of knowing and being.

Strong mission officers can help address this problem by convening the people already involved in cultivating Catholic character and identity, or who are at least interested in the project. By joining together, this critical mass of men and women can strengthen

---

"We become fully human when we become more than human, when we let God bring us beyond ourselves in order to attain the fullest truth of our being." (*Evangelii Gaudium*, 8)

· · · · · · · · · · · · · · · · · · · · · · · · · · · · · · ·

their personal commitment. They can also develop their cooperative spirit and activity, and increase the visibility and importance of their work in Catholic integration.

Many newer members of the faculty community are willing, if not eager, to contribute to the Catholic character and mission of the college or university they serve. They are far more likely to develop that interest if they can identify a like-minded group of faculty, staff, and administrators with whom they can work and from whom they can gain advice and support. Both formal and informal mentoring initiatives at some Catholic colleges and universities bring new faculty members into such a community early on in their careers.

Mission officers work with faculty and staff across departments and divisions as they formulate proposals and develop programs that enhance Catholic identity. An excellent way to invigorate this programmatic effort is to convene a Catholic audit, which includes the academic sector, goes beyond the theology department, and extends across divisions.

Individual audits of each department or division can be conducted by the mission officer or by an outside group with Catholic auditing experience. An external group can provide a fresh look at mission issues and—after spending a good deal of time with faculty, staff, and members of the campus community—can share valuable insights and suggestions about possible ways to proceed. Such audits serve two distinct purposes: they can uncover exactly what is happening on campus as it relates to the religious mission, and they can awaken interest about additional activities within their area that could be undertaken to advance the Catholic mission.

All of these efforts are important to consider and include, as they add depth and breadth to the institution's Catholic mission. Another advantage of convening an audit, especially if it is being done by an outside group, is that the mission officer sets the terms of engagement, working collaboratively with the auditors and retaining final decision-making authority.

## Catholic Cultural Conscience

There is a multitude of pressures on Catholic institutions as they compete in the educational marketplace. In order to appeal to a broader range of constituents, it can be tempting to soft-pedal the institution's Catholic character in order to cultivate the interest of individuals and groups who are indifferent or even suspicious of things Catholic. It is also true that Catholic institutions can err in the other direction, burnishing their Catholic *bona fides* despite providing meager opportunities for students to engage the Catholic Intellectual Tradition in the classroom and in student life. Institutions can easily get carried away with their own promotional material, resulting in an idealized view of what is happening on campus, rather than one that accurately reflects Catholic culture on the ground.

"The Son of God, by becoming flesh, summoned us to the revolution of tenderness." (*Evangelii Gaudium*, 88)

Mission officers cannot fall into this trap. Instead, they must operate as the conscience of the institution, prudently telling the true story, warts and all, about how the institution is measuring up to its stated ideals and goals. If the integration of faith and reason is happening only in the theology department, the mission officer should be relentless in reminding the administration and faculty that more has to be done. If there is little or no Catholic character to residence life and student affairs, the mission officer must raise concerns internally and persistently work for a different approach. By raising mission issues and suggesting initiatives, mission officers consistently remind the community to be attentive to and engaged with the institution's Catholic identity.

There are many competing demands on all Catholic college and university campuses. In the thrust and parry of academic life, it is easy for the religious mission of the institution to be overlooked. Mission officers must work to ensure this does not happen. Clearly they cannot do this work alone. However, they can make a significant contribution to the Catholic character, culture, mission, and identity of the institution they serve. They will do so if they catalyze Catholic culture, regularly convene a critical mass of individuals who are committed to and involved in the work of religious integration, and accept the role of serving as their institutions' Catholic cultural conscience.

*Melanie M. Morey is Provost at St. Patrick's Seminary and University, Menlo Park, CA.*

## chapter TWELVE
● ● ● ● ● ●

### The Mission Officer as Catholic Conscience on Campus

*Most Rev. David M. O'Connell, CM*

Ever since the publication of Pope John Paul II's apostolic constitution on Catholic universities, *Ex corde Ecclesiae*, on August 15, 1990, the phrase "Catholic identity and mission" has become part of the recurring vocabulary and conversation on Catholic university and college campuses. As a former Catholic university president, I have often defined that expression in this way: "who we are and what we do." The latter flows from the former, and the former motivates and enables the latter. It was not that the notion of Catholic identity and mission was not present on Catholic campuses prior to 1990. It was, rather, a newer articulation of the essence of Catholic higher education from the highest authority in the Church that helped focus the conversation following the Second Vatican Council (1963–65) and the revised Code of Canon Law (1983). And it did not hurt that Pope John Paul II was, himself, a university professor who knew the landscape well.

His successor, Pope Benedict XVI, also a former university professor and administrator, likewise displayed a great interest in the Catholic identity and mission of Catholic institutions of higher learning. During his only pastoral visit to the United States, Pope Benedict XVI chose to address Catholic educators gathered on the campus of The Catholic University of America in Washington, D.C. (April 17, 2008). "Education is integral to the mission of the Church to proclaim the Good News," the Holy Father began. He spoke of Catholic university and college campuses as places "to encounter the living God who in Jesus Christ reveals his *transforming* love and truth."

This transformative character and dimension of Catholic higher education is not something that happens just because a university or college claims to be Catholic. No, transformation is intentional and deliberate, a slow but steady process; it happens because administrators, faculty, and staff on Catholic campuses work at it—through teaching and the creation of a supportive Catholic environment—and because students on Catholic campuses are open to and want it. Catholic identity is, indeed, who we are. Catholic mission is, indeed, what we do on the Catholic campus. They are the non-negotiables of a truly Catholic postsecondary educational experience.

In *Ex corde Ecclesiae*, Pope John Paul II reminded us that "the responsibility for maintaining and strengthening the Catholic identity of the university rests primarily with the university itself" (II, 4.1). Like his successor after him, Pope John Paul II viewed the Catholic university and college campus as a place to encounter Jesus Christ, a place for evangelization, a place where the Church can see its mission come to life. The late Holy Father recognized the distinct roles of various members of the Catholic university and college community as they contribute to the integration of the Church's mission with that of the Catholic university and college. In that community, Pope John Paul II noted that the local Church in the person of the diocesan bishop plays a significant role. "Even when they do not enter directly into the internal governance of the University, Bishops 'should be seen not as external agents but as participants in the life of the Catholic University'" (28). How that works in the concrete depends upon both the bishop concerned and the institutional authorities who, as *Ex corde Ecclesiae* states, should exist in a relationship of "communion with the universal Church … (and) the local Church (II, 5.1)," a relationship "characterized by mutual trust, close and consistent cooperation and continuing dialogue" (28).

St. Norbert College and the Catholic Diocese of Green Bay strengthen their relationship through regular meetings held throughout the year, administered by both the campus and diocesan leaders. These include: conversations between the bishop and the college's Religious Studies faculty and its Mission and Student Affairs staff; panel presentations on Catholic Intellectual Tradition by the bishop, president, and abbot of St. Norbert Abbey; meetings with the president, the bishop, the head of diocesan administration and the college's VP for Mission and Student Affairs; and a dialogue group of diocesan and college staff members.

Although it is primary and always essential that a healthy, positive relationship be developed and maintained between the president (and the board of trustees) of the Catholic university and college and the local bishop regarding the promotion of an institution's Catholic identity and mission, recent decades have witnessed the appointment of a mission officer to help the Catholic campus maintain its identity, character and mission. The mission officer may be, but is usually not, a faculty member and, therefore, does not enter directly into the development and content of curriculum which is, of course,

"...[W]e need to provide an education which teaches critical thinking and encourages the development of mature moral values." (*Evangelii Gaudium*, 64)

the prerogative of the faculty. He or she, however, should be thoroughly conversant with what is being taught and presented on campus as Catholic teaching, theology, or doctrine, enough that he or she can articulate clearly and accurately how the institution's academic mission and the Church's mission to evangelize relate to and support one another. Although the mission officer most often reports directly to the president, his or her role should be publicly supportive of, and available to, the faculty's efforts to teach what the Church teaches: to teach the truth.

A mission officer is not a chaplain or campus minister, but his or her relationship with individuals so designated or appointed is critically important since the chaplain or campus minister is the administrator who usually has the most direct, daily faith-related contact especially with, but not limited to, Catholic students outside of the classroom. They should never be or be perceived as rivals but, rather, as colleagues who collaborate together in witnessing to and sharing the Catholic faith, strengthening Catholic identity, and promoting the mission that flows from both. Similarly, a mission officer needs to work closely with student life personnel, also distinct from campus ministers, to foster the promotion of Catholic mission in the policies and practices of the Office of Student Life on campus. Here, as an administrator reporting to the president, a mission officer— without developing a reputation as a spy—can be an effective conduit of information to those with institutional responsibility for maintaining and implementing Catholic identity and mission throughout the institution, thereby enabling them to know what is happening on campus: those things that support institutional Catholicity and those things that work against it.

"Again and again, the Church has acted as a mediator in finding solutions to problems affecting peace, social harmony, the land, the defence of life, human and civil rights, and so forth. And how much good has been done by Catholic schools and universities around the world! This is a good thing. Yet, we find it difficult to make people see that when we raise other questions less palatable to public opinion, we are doing so out of fidelity to precisely the same convictions about human dignity and the common good." (*Evangelii Gaudium*, 65)

Often enough, faculty and staff members are in need of formation and education in the areas of Catholic identity and mission, especially when the workforce draws from a population of other religious or faith backgrounds. Regardless of their particular denominational affiliation or lack of one, faculty and staff members have an obligation to support the identity and mission of a Catholic university and college. A mission officer can be an extremely effective help in this regard. He or she can provide faculty and staff orientations at the beginning of their employment and periodically during its continuation. The mission officer's service can and should be non-threatening to employees who might be unfamiliar with the Catholic Church and its teachings and practices. Occasional retreats, days of recollection, or professional development can take advantage of employees' service.

Although university and college presidents are the primary institutional contacts with boards of trustees, a mission officer can be of tremendous assistance to the president and chairperson of the board by helping to vet potential trustee candidates (in confidence, of course) from the perspective of commitment to and support for Catholic identity. He or she can perform a similar service when it comes to candidates proposed for institutional honors such as honorary degrees or commencement speakers—again, in confidence. A mission officer can also assist the institution with the formation of the board in its awareness of Catholic identity and mission as they pertain to the Catholic university or college and the fiduciary responsibilities board members exercise. Too often, the fiduciary responsibilities of a board are viewed almost exclusively in terms of financial sustainability and campus growth. Boards are also responsible for effective oversight of the institution's Catholic identity and mission, an equally important fiduciary responsibility. A mission officer, working with the president and chairperson, can prepare retreats and other presentations to heighten the board's awareness of its Catholic mission-related obligations, an important part of a board's orientation and development.

The role of a mission officer at a Catholic university and college is a work in progress, a relatively recently developed administrative position. He or she is "neither fish nor flesh"—ordinarily not a faculty member, nor a chaplain, nor a student life professional—working in a class by himself or herself, yet, whose mission work touches virtually every dimension of Catholic campus life. In a very real sense, the mission officer can, and perhaps should, be the Catholic conscience of the Catholic university and college campus.

Pope John Paul II reflected in *Ex corde Ecclesiae* that "by its very nature, each Catholic University makes an important contribution to the Church's work of evangelization. It is a living *institutional* witness to Christ and his message, so vitally important in cultures marked by secularism, or where Christ and his message are still virtually unknown" (49). That notion must be part of the job description of a mission officer, exercised appropriately and collaboratively with all his or her colleagues who strive to make and keep the university and college Catholic at all levels of an institution's existence.

Having served as a Catholic university president for many years and, now, as a diocesan bishop, I can see the great value added to an institution's Catholic environment and ethos by a deeply committed and effective mission officer. The job and responsibility for mission is too important for it not to be intentionally incorporated into an institution's structure. At the same time, however, the job and responsibility for mission cannot be left to a single administrator. Catholic identity and mission is everyone's responsibility at a Catholic university and college. A mission officer can and should be a positive institutional resource to keep that responsibility before everyone's mind and heart on campus.

*Most Reverend David M. O'Connell, CM is President Emeritus of The Catholic University of America and Bishop of Trenton, Trenton, NJ.*

## chapter THIRTEEN

## Integrating Mission through Empowerment and Teamwork

*Leona Misto, RSM*

The university mission is the heart of the life of the Salve Regina University community. Integrating mission through collaboration empowers all segments of a university campus as well as the community in which it resides. Success of mission integration is grounded in the practice of inviting faculty, staff, and students to be part of the process for designing and executing programs. This empowerment model encourages ownership, teaches the mission, and effectively integrates it throughout the university. Most of all, programming designed and implemented in this manner proved effective and life-giving to all members of the Salve Regina University community. This chapter will offer eight ideas for mission integration.

A framed mission statement is prominently placed in every building on the Salve Regina University campus, and there is a crucifix in each classroom.

### Connect Mission to Departmental Goals and Objectives

First, it was necessary to have the entire community understand and commit to the mission, before it could be comprehensively integrated. The strategic planning process began by engaging all departments in creating specific goals and objectives relating to mission and the values of the founding order, the Sisters of Mercy. There was a mid-year review of the progress of each goal and a year-end assessment as well.

### Develop Faculty Using a Collegium Method

The next initiative was to secure funding for several faculty members to attend the eight-day national *Collegium* sponsored by the Association of Catholic Colleges and Universities for faculty teaching at Catholic institutions. In subsequent years, other faculty attended the *Collegium* and engaged in discussions related to preserving the Catholic identity of the institution and enlivening its religious traditions.

The result was a shortened version of the *Collegium*. It is offered on campus annually and consists of an overnight program with the objective of introducing faculty to Catholic identity, Mercy values, and Catholic Social Teaching. Seventy percent of the faculty has participated in at least one Collegium. Professional personnel and other staff participate in half-day programs with the same objectives.

## Establish a VP Position for Mission Integration and Planning

Understanding the mission and integrating it throughout an institution requires commitment at a university's highest levels. Salve Regina University created a senior administrative position, Vice President for Mission Integration and Planning, whose responsibilities include managing the university's planning process and the development of policies and programs ensuring consistency with the university mission. The vice president also interviews all prospective faculty hires to ensure that they understand the concepts of the university mission and are aware of their obligation to support its tenets.

At Salve Regina University, mission integration grants of up to $500 are available to faculty, staff, and students for creating a project that integrates a mission principle into the work of their department or activity.

As part of the strategic planning process the vice president is responsible for promoting and maintaining both Catholic identity and Mercy values. The mission is the foundation of all planning, and in that process it is essential to establish a strong vision statement and mission-centered university goals. All departmental goals and steps in the strategic plan flow from the mission statement, which was approved by the Board of Trustees, and are incorporated in the vision statement and university goals.

### Mission Integration

While it is essential to have a comprehensive mission statement that faculty, staff, and students understand, the mission must be fully and properly integrated into the works of the university. A university mission committee was formed, composed of faculty and staff, charged with assessing the implementation of the university mission into the academic and co-curricular programs and increasing awareness of mission-related issues.

## Conduct a Survey

The mission committee developed a university-wide mission survey, the results of which are reviewed, collated, and published annually on the university website. Board members, faculty, staff, and students each develop a Mission Effectiveness Statement. These statements identify aspects of the mission the group choose to promote. For example, board members agreed to practice good stewardship by exercising fiscal responsibility in their decisions. Staff members strove to become stewards of the university's future by engaging

At Salve Regina University, the Chartres Replica labyrinth was constructed in the center of campus to remind each passerby to take time for reflection and prayer.

and supporting students. The surveys serve as reminders of ways each group integrates the mission on a daily basis.

## Advance an Environmental Sustainability Plan

In keeping with the mission statement, the university set Environmental Sustainability Goals to create an environmentally literate and responsible community. These goals were implemented by establishing a major in Environmental Studies. Goals embedded in the major are fostering faculty and student research on sustainable development, working with the Aquidneck Watershed Project, developing a student-operated hydroponic garden, conserving water by installing filtered water dispensers and limiting bottled water, reducing waste with tray-less dining, initiating use of free public transportation for students, and promoting a bicycle lease program on campus. Salve Regina is a member of the Catholic Coalition on Climate sponsored by the ACCU and the USCCB.

Department heads from facilities, grounds, dining, and housekeeping services, along with faculty and students, work diligently to achieve the sustainability goals. The Vice President for Mission Integration chairs the University Environmental Committee and acts as liaison to the Staff/Faculty Environmental Committee and the Student Environment Club to ensure all are working in harmony to be good stewards of God's creation.

New Student Seminar advisors at Salve Regina University incorporate the mission into the first-year seminar through readings and service-learning projects connected to mission objectives. First-year students publicly recite the Student Mission Effectiveness Pledge at the annual Fall Convocation.

## Initiate Mission Orientation Programs

Orientation programs provide another venue for educating the community about Catholic and Mercy traditions. Programs are prepared for new members of the Board of Trustees, faculty, staff and students. Although programs differ, all focus on the university mission as it relates to Catholic identity and Mercy distinction. All participants receive a calligraphic copy of the mission statement and other materials related to the mission. Specific orientation programs are prepared annually as part of the training for residence assistants, student orientation leaders, and the New Student Seminar advisors and mentors.

## Promote Use of the Chapel and Spiritual Symbols

The chapel is the central place for the university to promote its Catholic identity by celebrating the sacraments and providing instruction for initiation into the sacraments of Baptism and Confirmation. Daily celebration of the Eucharist is open to everyone. The chaplain provides the sacrament of Reconciliation and coordinates arrangements for Catholic marriages in the chapel. The chapel bells, which ring throughout the day, remind all of God's presence.

## Strengthen Campus Ministry

The Campus Ministry Office, known as Mercy Center for Spiritual Life, shares a building with the chapel, and is a welcome haven to students of all beliefs. It houses five offices, four separate seating areas, and a large kitchen. Students gather for study, lunch, or spiritual support. A training program prepares student leaders for the center. A group called "Mercy in Motion" plans weekly activities that explore dimensions of faith and spirituality. They promote hospitality by helping with move-in

_____

**The Salve Regina Mission Committee periodically sponsors university-wide programs and noon-time lectures, which help to build awareness of the mission.**

• • • • • • • • • • • • • • • • • • • • • • • • • • • • • • • •

day for new students and other activities. The staff offers student retreats, various prayer experiences, the RCIA program, and community service projects that advance the social justice teachings of the Catholic Church.

The Director of the center reports directly to the Vice President for Mission Integration for purposes of program planning and policies. The center's staff works independently but is in frequent communication with the vice president. Meetings are held regularly to establish goals, set objectives, refine the budget, and review the work of Mercy Center.

These programs, opportunities, and initiatives are part of the means to bring about the transformation envisioned in the mission. Every member of the community is empowered to work for a world that is harmonious, just and merciful by having the opportunity to acquire a deeper understanding of the university mission.

*Sr. Leona Misto, RSM is Vice President for Mission Integration at Salve Regina University, Newport, RI.*

## chapter FOURTEEN

## The Mission Officer and "The Mission Officer President"

*Maryellen Gilroy*
*Lorraine Sloma-Williams*
*Michael Galligan-Stierle*

This chapter will address the role of the president at a Catholic college university when there is and is not a mission officer. It will identify ways in which both situations can be highly effective in establishing and fostering a vibrant Catholic identity and integrated Catholic mission.

The university's board of directors holds in trust the Catholic identity and university mission distinguished by its diocesan, religious order, or lay founding. They hire and hold accountable the president for the university's mission and its Catholic identity. Although the president retains full accountability for mission—similar to the way in which a president appoints a vice president of finance although he or she still remains responsible for the fiscal health of the institution—he or she most often hires a mission officer who becomes a significant part of the institution's organizational structure. However, there are cases where the president does not appoint a mission officer (20 percent).[1] In this case, the president may expand and envelop mission priorities and duties into his or her responsibilities, or may prefer to see these tasks as part of the director of campus ministry or university chaplain's portfolio. In all cases, clear identification of oneself or another as the mission officer is helpful to the university community.

### Institutions with a Mission Officer

In 80 percent of Association of Catholic Colleges and Universities (ACCU) member institutions, a mission officer is actively engaged to advance and lead Catholic mission priorities on campus. In 89 percent of cases, the mission officer reports directly to the president (*Mission Matters*, James, et al., 2010). He or she typically has an operating budget, works with cabinet-level administrators, and involves faculty, staff, and students in advancing the mission and charism of the university.

Having a designated mission officer has several advantages affecting the president's role. For example, the mission officer makes it his or her priority to ensure that mission questions are raised in all institutional decisions, thereby freeing the president from having to ensure that such conversations occur. A mission officer also fields many Catholic identity questions from external audiences, alleviating the president of this task. The

---

1  *As of 2012, there were 159 mission officers at ACCU's 200 member institutions, 80 percent.*

mission officer can assist other departments or offices to make mission a priority without compromising other important areas such as academic excellence, student retention, and fiscal health of the institution. By designating a mission officer, the president has a mechanism to address mission in a systematic way across all areas of the institution. Creating an outcomes assessment tool in this regard can be very beneficial.

Catholic identity and university mission are best advanced when a collaborative relationship exists between the mission officer and the president. For instance, the president can invite the mission officer to be part of strategic discussions involving mission integration across the entire institution. Likewise, the mission officer may involve the president in mission-related activities, either directly or through soliciting input. Both mission officer and president should be selected for their respective positions in part because they each have a strong passion and knowledge of the mission. Thus, they can be excellent allies for one another, as they both seek to strengthen and articulate the mission.

Mission officers and presidents may not always be the best of allies. Examples could be a reporting structure that places the mission officer outside of significant decision-making conversations, inadequate program funding levels, or lack of clarity about expected outcomes. Clearly, the mission officer is most effective when he or she has the encouragement and blessing of the president to ensure that all campus members have a clear understanding of the mission and the contributions to mission they might make. All are needed to participate in creating transformative learning experiences for students and offering enriching mission opportunities for faculty and staff.

## Campuses without Mission Officers

In 20 percent of ACCU institutions, there is not an appointed mission officer. Reasons for not having a designated mission officer vary. For instance, some presidents did invest in appointing mission officers in good faith, yet they did not yield positive results. Because of this reality, the president is now reluctant or believes time must pass before the institution hires a new mission officer. A member of the sponsoring religious congregation may have been appointed who was the living embodiment of the charism; however, he or she may have not been able to meet the demands of the office or did not have the necessary credentials to succeed. Some institutions are simply unable to make the financial investment necessary for another administrative position. In other institutions, the president considers mission leadership an integral component of his or her presidency and, thus, prefers to keep this important duty.

When there is not a mission officer, the president typically assumes many of the tasks that would reside with a mission officer and assigns some of the mission officer responsibilities to senior and mid-level staff, the director of campus ministry, or the university chaplain. In these cases, the president retains the primary responsibility but asks others to pay special attention to integrating mission priorities across

At Ave Maria University, a lay-initiated university, the campus minister is in part the mission officer. While the lay president ensures that the strategic plan is mission-centric and mission occupies a central role in hiring and retention, the campus minister is a member of the University Council precisely to bring to bear questions of mission on the Catholic culture of the university.

campus. Thus, the president is primarily responsible for animating the mission and values of the organization in addition to his or her regular duties as president. This expansion is often a natural fit for the president; by virtue of his or her unique background and repertoire of knowledge and skills, he or she can cultivate and promote Catholic identity and university mission in very thoughtful ways, and others can then attend to implementation.

This option provides several advantages. Presidents are privy to all cabinet-level meetings and decisions. They are closely involved with strategic planning, thereby influencing long-term sustainability of mission integration. With their oversight of the budget, they have discretion over how funds are allocated. In addition, when the president assumes responsibilities that would otherwise go to a mission officer, there is no need to spend energy "convincing the president" that mission is important. The president can use his or her position to articulate the unity of Church and university mission, to convey to all constituents the relevance of the Catholic mission (including potential donors), and to engage the board and the sponsoring religious congregation, if present.

Although there are advantages, there is a significant challenge for the president when he or she assumes the tasks of the mission officer. With the increasing complexity of the demands of presidents, (e.g., fundraising, engaging the community, and working with the board) focusing on the day-to-day realities of creating an integrated mission program and well-articulated Catholic identity on campus may be impractical.

Siena College's president belongs to the same religious congregation that sponsors the college. The presence of a Franciscan friar to lead the organization is a visible reminder to all of the institutional mission and history. The president demonstrates that Franciscanism is "caught not taught," and it is the lived experience of those who work or study at Siena College.

• • • • • • • • • • • • • • • • • • • • • • • • • • • • • • •

In situations where the president is part of the sponsoring religious congregation (as is the case in 32 percent of all ACCU institutions), the priest or religious order president has a special link to the founding charism of the institution. There is an intimate understanding of the values, practices, and traditions that define the congregation and that these presidents bring to the presidency. Thus, when an institution has as its president a member of the sponsoring religious congregation, the institution could *intentionally* opt for the president to assume the duties of mission officer. This situation could be a good mission fit, and the president may be a natural embodiment of the institution's Catholic mission. However, as the institutional landscape changes and more lay individuals take on the role of the presidency, special care should be taken by trustees to hire a lay president with the right skill set, commitment, and experience to lead effectively, both as president and mission leader. In all cases, whether lay or religious, the person hired must be comfortable and credentialed so as to ensure that mission remains central to the purpose of the institution.

## Presidents as Icons of the University's Mission

Presidents should be active and effective leaders of their institutional missions, whether a university has a mission officer or not. They are responsible to articulate the mission and engage the community from their unique vantage point, regardless of their life choice of lay, religious order, or priest. As presidents, they are often called upon to engage in specific Catholic identity and university mission leadership activities such as: educating the university community about mission; telling the founder's story; collaborating in enhancing academic priorities that advance the Catholic Intellectual Tradition and liberal arts education; fostering education that integrates personal aspirations and spiritual growth with academic achievements; participating

The Siena College Strategic Plan features both the Franciscan and Catholic mission. Through it, the president encourages the college community to ensure students are exposed to mission-centric experiences. At each Cabinet meeting, the president leads a discussion on mission. His influence as the institutional mission officer permeates employee orientation, service trips for students, and speaking events on and off campus.

in and promoting campus ministry and service-learning programs; affirming mission orientation initiatives for employees and students; and encouraging periodic retreats and seminars for trustees. In all cases, the president will be seen as a living icon of the university's mission and the charism of the institution.

## Conclusion

Advancing university mission and Catholic identity varies from institution to institution, whether an institution designates a specific individual within the organizational structure as the mission officer, or the president keeps the primary responsibility to him or herself. Each institution needs to assess the challenge of how to appropriately keep Catholic identity and university mission distinctive to that institution. There are advantages and challenges to each approach. Regardless of the location within the organizational structure, it is clear that wherever the responsibility rests, skill, commitment, and a collaborative spirit are essential.

*Maryellen Gilroy is Vice President for Student Affairs at Siena College, Loudonville, NY.*

*Lorraine Sloma-Williams is an independent consultant with Ancoris Consulting, LLC, Falls Church, VA.*

*Michael Galligan-Stierle is President of the Association of Catholic Colleges and Universities, Washington, DC.*

## chapter FIFTEEN

## The President's Choice of a Mission Officer: Able to Frame Hard Questions, Live with Contradiction, and Stand in the Tension

*Graziano Marcheschi*
*Christine Wiseman*

The times in which we live generally dictate the kind of person who can best respond to predominant issues and needs. So it is with the university president's choice of a mission officer. At a time when "Catholic identity" has no comprehensive single definition or uniform set of tenets among the leaders of Catholic colleges and universities, the vagaries have created political as well as social controversy. Especially in these times, university presidents are best served by mission officers who are well versed in Catholic Intellectual Tradition and the history of Catholic Social Teaching—but who also can deal with uncertainty, are not intransigent, and are not unnerved by difficult questions that elude easy answers. Equipped with these attributes, the mission officer becomes a unique resource person for the president in the president's interaction with all campus constituencies—students, staff, faculty, and even alumni—especially in matters of social policy.

The social and demographic landscape in Catholic higher education has changed dramatically over the years; near certainties in former times are "givens" no more. With percentages of Catholic students and faculty members on a campus continuing to decline, consensus around identity and mission is often more difficult to attain. Greater diversity, coupled with a tenuous Catholic "majority" on campus, sometimes becomes a mandate to speak "less Catholic" and to substitute "values" or "social justice" language for "God" language. When there are fewer commonly held convictions and fewer constituents who hold them, the ability to send a clear and consistent message is sometimes

---

Today's mission officer is called upon to help navigate a significant number of Catholic identity and university mission questions, including: "How does a president or mission officer pose to candidates who are of another faith tradition or no faith tradition the Catholic identity and academic freedom question?" "Should additional scholarship monies be allocated to Catholic high school graduates or Catholic parishioners in a desire to increase the student Catholic presence?" And "How might the art and artifacts on campus give shape to Catholic identity and the tradition of the founding religious community?"

•  •  •  •  •  •  •  •  •  •  •  •  •  •  •  •  •  •  •  •  •  •  •  •  •  •  •  •  •  •

compromised. Effective leadership is therefore charged more than ever with the task of *framing the questions* for the university community—for resident students, commuter students, faculty, and staff. Knowing that consensus will be elusive, the mission officer must find ways of initiating the conversation with and within the community. And the key to his or her success will be knowing what questions to ask on a given campus, at this particular moment in its history, and within the unique mix of circumstances that distinguish its life. A mission officer also needs to understand and value the Catholic Intellectual Tradition both in its breadth and in its particularity. Catholic thought has made many and significant contributions to society. The value of some of those contributions goes unquestioned. But other insights and intuitions, those "hard sayings" that get at the unique core of the Church's mission in the world, those do not gain currency within contemporary culture. Some of those insights, in fact, are decidedly countercultural and serve to challenge the status quo. Whether those are insights regarding

> "If need be, a Catholic University must have the courage to speak uncomfortable truths which do not please public opinion, but which are necessary to safeguard the authentic good of society." (*Ex corde Ecclesiae*, 32)

social issues or issues of personal morality and piety, the Catholic Intellectual Tradition has more than enough in its archives to trouble the thinkers of any generation. It is not enough for a mission officer to be steeped in those values on which we would all agree—service, respect, diversity, excellence; he or she also must acquire fluency in those areas about which there will be controversy and dissension, perhaps even outright rejection. To be successful in this engagement, the mission officer must be open, comfortable in dialogue with others, and willing to engage members of the university community where they are—not necessarily where he or she would like them to be.

Equally important, at a Catholic institution that is also a university community, an effective mission officer will know the Church—even though a worldwide, two-thousand-year-old institution is not easily knowable. There are institutional, doctrinal, liturgical, and spiritual dimensions of the life of the Church, each with its own vast body of knowledge. Dogma, doctrine, and discipline are distinctively different concepts as well.

> "Differing currents of thought in philosophy, theology and pastoral practice, if open to being reconciled by the Spirit in respect and love, can enable the Church to grow, since all of them help to express more clearly the immense riches of God's word." (*Evangelii Gaudium*, 40)

Given that a Catholic university may be home to experts within each of those fields of inquiry, a mission officer cannot be a credible partner in dialogue with all of them if he or she lacks basic fluency in these areas of Church life. But fluency alone is not likely to be sufficient. Especially important to a president, the effective mission officer will know how to create opportunities for dialogue among all these university colleagues in order to foster joint ownership of the larger university mission goals that often transcend disciplinary interests.

And since a mission officer focuses on "mission," he or she also must understand what motivated the founders and what led them to establish the particular institution. For the founders of our Catholic institutions, the question of what stoked the fire of their passion inevitably leads to Jesus Christ. The founders of Catholic institutions did what they did—whether it was to build monasteries or schools, hospitals or orphanages, universities or chapels—in the name of Christ and to serve his people. A mission officer will need to deal with that truth and do so in a way that respects the diversity of the many faith traditions likely to occupy Catholic institutions, without denying the legacy that gave them life.

"Born from the heart of the Church, a Catholic University is located in that course of tradition which may be traced back to the very origin of the University as an institution. It has always been recognized as an incomparable centre of creativity…" (*Ex corde Ecclesiae*, 1)

Though founded on Christ, the legacy of the named founders has a life of its own. Valuing that legacy means that a mission officer will seek ways to dedicate time, energy, passion, and creativity to exploring the message of the founders and to finding new means of incarnating that legacy in the present milieu. In short, the mission must continue to thrive in the present day and the present culture. But founders were *innovators*, and so the mission officer also must be committed to innovation. The founders typically pushed boundaries, risked failure, forged alliances, and stood alone when necessary. Mission officers must be people willing and able to do the same. Mission, especially in times of declining university operational margins, often represents the *cutting edge* of an institution and its programs—the single most distinctive feature from which even contemporary notions of institutional accreditation and assessment will follow. Anyone afraid to bleed a little best not apply.

At the same time, mission officers must be individuals of honesty and integrity who do not confuse their own agendas for that of the founders. More than once the "vision of the founders" has been used to justify decisions that contradict or abandon the very vision and legacy they purport to foster. Mission is everyone's responsibility, and strategic plans increasingly must reflect that accountability; accreditors seek that ownership paradigm, and the president and mission officer must seek it as well.

Ultimately, of course, nothing exists in a vacuum. So an effective mission officer also must *understand* the culture that occupies and surrounds the educational institution he or she serves. With a discerning eye, the mission officer will value what is good and helpful within the culture and work with the president to transform what is unhelpful or destructive. He or she will understand that truth exists everywhere, within all cultures, and will seek ways to spotlight and support those aspects that are "growthful" and good.

Most of all, the mission officer must be a person of contradiction. He or she cannot be a hybrid or a compromiser but must be someone who holds opposing truths in tension. As G. K. Chesterton long ago commented in his chapter on "The Paradoxes of Christianity" (*Orthodoxy*, 1908):

> [t]he historic church has at once emphasised celibacy and emphasised the family; … It has kept them side by side like two strong colours,

> red and white, like the red and white upon the shield of St. George.
> … It hates that combination of two colours which is the feeble
> expedient of the philosophers. It hates that evolution of black into
> white which is tantamount to a dirty grey.

Chesterton's point, of course, is that the Church refuses to blend truths in a way that results in the dilution of both.

There are many truths that stand on opposite poles but become equal partners in fashioning the path by which people live their lives; these cannot be reconciled or homogenized, nor should they. Justice and mercy come readily to mind; each has its place and each demands consideration. And, of course, there are others that mark human nature. We are sinners and we are saved; we are both *"curvatus in se"* (bent in on the self) and yet an *"imago Dei,"* (an image of God); we are made good and yet incline toward evil. We hold and value these opposing truths because none alone tells the whole story. All the mission officer can do is hold these truths in tension, with confidence that only in knowing both will he or she have the capacity to deal with what is and help forge what should be.

*Graziano Marcheschi is Executive Director, Office for University Mission and Ministry at Saint Xavier University, Chicago, IL.*

*Christine Wiseman is President of Saint Xavier University, Chicago, IL.*

## chapter SIXTEEN

## Mission Integration and the Board of Trustees: Formation for Transformational Leadership

*David McCallum, SJ*

### Introduction

Every institutional mission exists in a wider and often complex social and economic context. Cultural trends are shifting away from personal identification with religious institutions and transcendent values in the direction of secular materialism and a reductionist orientation. Crises in the global economy, demographic downturns in numbers of college-age students, and disruptive changes in online learning are challenging leaders of religiously affiliated institutions, including boards of trustees, to devote greater attention to the Catholic and charism-based mission of their schools and to the way that mission guides executive decision making. A transactional management style may have once been sufficient for trustees as they executed their fiduciary responsibilities on behalf of their institutions, but no longer. New and emerging challenges call board members to lead the adaptation and evolution of their institutions while at the same time deepening commitment to their mission. Successful institutional adaptation requires a transformational leadership style that inquires into operating assumptions, revises core strategies, and inspires a higher level of organizational performance.

Board members, whether they are Catholic or not, are called to exercise a transformational style in their internal and external leadership roles, to work with presidents, executive teams, staff, and faculty to inspire an institutional ethos that reflects deeper commitment to the vision and values of Catholic higher education, and to motivate both professional morale and performance. The effectiveness of transformational leadership depends on the values and priorities of individual trustees, grounded in faith-based education of the whole person and academic excellence oriented toward service of the common good. The leadership role of mission officers often includes active engagement with the board of trustees, with the chair of the board, the chair of the mission committee, and the committee itself. The reflection that follows will explore practical ways of building this transformational leadership capacity through board formation and the particular functions the board's mission committee might serve.

## Formation for Transformational Board Leadership

Collaborative transformational leadership requires boards to work with administration and faculty to present a compelling, value-based education rooted in the Catholic tradition, while also open to diversity and practical for the times. Board members with knowledge and appreciation of the essential traits of Catholic higher education can confidently express these values to a public that is suspicious of liberal arts and seeks both lower costs for education and efficient tracks to post-graduation employment.

This shift requires board members to have an informed knowledge of the Catholic Intellectual Tradition, the charism of the founding orders (where applicable), and the particular qualities of the institutional mission that distinguish it from other schools. These areas of content knowledge can be shaped into learning objectives for board orientations and guide the development of assessment tools for board members. For example, early in their service, do board members understand the essential aspects of the mission of Catholic higher education and have a basic familiarity with key documents, such as *Ex corde Ecclesiae*? Later in their service, are they confident in their ability to articulate and champion their school's mission to external audiences, including donors and foundations? To effectively engage and help transform the dominant cultures, both inside and outside Catholic institutions, board members must demonstrate their knowledge and their conviction that Catholic higher education is an essential and value-adding feature of the educational landscape.

A transformational leader is able to tell the story of his or her institutional mission in a way that inspires, motivates, uplifts, and illustrates this mission through the unmistakable authenticity of his or her own lived example. Informational learning alone does not foster this kind of leadership. Such formation for boards requires both information and transformational elements in order to reach the degree of substance and depth called for in transformational leadership. Informational elements are easier to deliver in the form of introductory readings supplied to board candidates during the period in which they are vetted by governance committees, as well as in orientations for new members, and in mission-oriented modules scheduled each time the board gathers. While some universities will use online and video-based materials for such informational purposes, these have less impact than face-to-face meetings to discuss and reflect with mission officers, college personnel, students, alumni, and fellow board members. Combinations of online and face-to-face opportunities also can be helpful.

> At Le Moyne College, the Mission & Identity Committee of the Board is designing a board formation model that will begin with areas of content knowledge that determine objectives for new and more experienced members, and which will be staged over the course of several years of the board member's service.

Transformational elements of board formation involve experiential learning, and usually entail more investment of time, money, and personnel, but yield a greater depth of impact. Examples of such transformational formation include in-depth case-study work in groups, mission-related retreats, heritage tours in the footsteps of religious orders' founders, and combinations of such experiences in the form of pilgrimages, brief service immersion trips, and experiences shadowing current students. The most effective transformational experiences deepen knowledge and understanding, build community, and help board leaders translate mission in terms of the particular functions and roles they serve and the way they take up these roles on behalf of the institution. For colleges and universities living out the charism of religious orders, it is helpful if both the informational and transformational elements of mission formation are developed out of the distinct spirituality (Augustinian, Benedictine, Dominican, Franciscan, Jesuit, Marianist, etc.) and way of proceeding at the heart of the institution. In this way, board members can participate in the spiritual embodiment of the mission even as members of religious congregations seek to do the same.

A commitment to forming board members for mission might be worthwhile as an end in itself, yet the value of this investment is most evident in the quality of board members' service to the institution. A solid mission-related knowledge base empowers board members to offer more informed service in the internal fiduciary roles they serve in hiring presidents, maintaining and increasing institutional fiscal health in such a way that margin is linked to mission, safeguarding academic quality consistent with the standards of the Catholic Intellectual Tradition, and supporting efforts to enhance student life and development. This formation might best begin with a mutual partnership between chief mission officers and a core group of board members who serve on a mission committee.

## Functions of the Board Committee on Mission and the Mission Officer

Many institutions opt for a model of mission leadership that integrates mission across all the board's functional committees (academic affairs, student life, enrollment management, finance, institutional advancement, etc.). Mission awareness often begins with a handful of internal institutional officers and highly invested board members working hand in hand with the president and mission officer, or through a mission sub-committee. With the goal of building board members' capacity to serve as transformational leaders for mission, the purview of a board committee could include the creation and implementation of a board formation program, oversight of mission-related dimensions of the strategic plan, and fundraising for mission endowments. In the interest of long-term, sustainable capacity-building, the most significant role may be that of supporting ongoing formation in partnership with the mission officer.

At Le Moyne College, the Office of Mission & Identity uses a "mission integration map" to align institutional functions and operations in the service of mission-driven goals including: spiritual, intellectual, and professional formation; the development of a mission-inspired, intentional academic and organizational culture; and mission-aligned organizational structures, policies, and procedures.

How does the mission officer best strengthen the capacity of the board to lead in a mission-driven and transformational manner? First and foremost, the mission officer builds upon the diversity, gifts, and competencies of each board member. Mission officers need to be skillful at engaging each board member where they are, using appropriate means to help them further their appreciation of and commitment to the mission. Finally, in order to facilitate ongoing and sustainable board development, mission officers need to be able to work collaboratively with members, deepening trust through their credibility and competence, and the collegial and compassionate way in which they support and challenge the board.

**Conclusion**

In order to support Catholic institutions of higher education in the increasingly secular climate of the United States, board members need to be as much transformational leaders as they are fiduciary managers. As transformational leaders, board members inspire deepening commitment to the mission, vision, and values of Catholic higher education, both with their internal stakeholder responsibilities and as external spokespeople in society. In close partnership with chief mission officers and other internal stakeholders, board chairs and mission committees can help guide and enhance efforts at mission integration within the institution, offer orientation and ongoing formation for board members, and serve as champions for the unique contributions that Catholic institutions provide American higher education.

*Rev. David McCallum, SJ is Interim Dean, Madden School of Business and Director of Mission and Identity at Le Moyne College, Syracuse, NY.*

## chapter SEVENTEEN

## Mission Messaging: The Relationship between the Mission Officer and the Board of Trustees

*Donna Easton*
*Christine De Vinne, OSU*

Catholic colleges and universities are mission-driven institutions, and delivering the mission message with clarity, strength, and consistency is a vital means of promoting their identity. As the keepers of Catholic identity and university mission, each institution's board of trustees carries primary responsibility for this goal. The mission officer supports the university by serving the board and the president as a critical link in a chain of mission connections.

### Relationship with the Board and the President

At Notre Dame of Maryland University, the mission officer is a member of the School of Notre Dame, which gives her a unique relationship with the board of trustees. She educates, advises, and in some ways partners with them; however, the mission officer must remember that she, like all institutional administrators, reports to the president, who in turn reports to the board. The mission officer's challenge is to be accountable to the trustees, yet simultaneously teach and coach them in the mission responsibilities they oversee.

In both title and authority, the mission officer has been appointed by the president, who also stands in a special relationship to the board. Both on and off campus, with internal and external constituencies, the president is the institution's chief spokesperson for the mission and, with senior leadership, holds responsibility for voicing and living that mission. In good measure, the board can judge the effectiveness of the mission officer by how successfully she enables the president and other representatives to speak of and act upon the mission. The mission officer's work of education and acculturation begins with the president.

At the same time, the mission officer plays a crucial role in educating the board, both individually and collectively. The mission officer is a primary participant in every new trustee's orientation, including thoughtful explanation and discussion of each component of the university's mission statement. In these interactions, the mission officer is not only the tutor but the student as well. Through conversation on each point of the mission, the mission officer gains an appreciation for what new trustees bring to the institution. Only through their engagement, as they embrace and claim the mission as their own, will the university be successful in promoting its Catholic identity. The mission officer recognizes that responsibility for the board's understanding of the congregational mission lies with the chair of the board and the president of the university, in partnership with the mission officers of the congregation.

The mission officer not only helps integrate new members but is also expected to provide ongoing board education. Directly and indirectly, the mission officer exercises a wide span of influence. In continuous and focused ways, trustees are enriched by inviting the mission officer to collaborate in guided discussions at board meetings, mission reflections, and mission-focused retreats. Led by the board chair, the mission officer helps ensure that the mission is embedded in every aspect of the board's work. Especially in strategic planning, the mission officer should review the elements of the mission with everyone involved, so that all objectives, strategies, and tactics flow from and back to the mission. Whenever the institution recognizes a need to revise or update its mission statement, the mission officer can serve a key role in immersing board members in the full meaning of institutional mission.

Recognizing their significant role as the primary "keepers of the mission," trustees need the guidance of the mission officer throughout any search for a new president. In such a transition, the mission officer must collaborate with the board, the search committee, and any outside search firm in establishing selection criteria for serious candidates. Among those criteria, embracing the mission of the university and that of the sponsoring congregation must be clearly articulated as a priority. Bringing a discerning eye to candidates' resumes, the mission officer looks for evidence that their backgrounds have prepared them for consistent, committed service to mission. The mission officer is also an active participant with the search committee in reviewing and interviewing finalists. This early engagement with the candidates, particularly the ultimate nominee, is key in bringing the best qualified new president on board and establishing a trusted relationship as the foundation for learning and living the mission.

> Trustees utilize an online computer program consisting of e-notes, a two-minute video, and a short resource prior to meetings at Xavier University. Trustees find the six-part seminar time-efficient and user-friendly with topics relevant to their roles and responsibilities in promoting and maintaining the university's mission and the Jesuit Catholic tradition. http://www.xavier.edu/mission-identity/trustees/index.cfm

> At Notre Dame of Maryland University (NDMU), the position of mission officer was established in 2002 especially to educate and assist the new president in becoming the primary voice of mission and institutional identity.

A new president needs deep grounding in the mission in order to assume his or her leadership role with the board and all other constituents. A close relationship between the mission officer and the president enables such mission leadership throughout a presidential term.

## Responsibilities to the Board in Guiding Faculty and Staff

At NDMU, the president and mission officer meet frequently, both formally and informally. Together with the rest of the executive leadership team, they effectively constitute a mission and identity committee. The mission officer's influence is extended on campus through various standing and *ad hoc* committees. In 2002, the president and chair for academic affairs inaugurated the Catholic Intellectual Life Committee. The mission officer lends support to this standing faculty committee. Such internal structures, like the mission committee of a board, support the mission officer in sharing the mission message throughout campus.

Regular updates are essential for the board in its responsibility to ensure that deans, chairs, and faculty have the support they need to direct the mission-driven intellectual life of the university. Under the guidance of the mission officer, not only do trustees support processes that hire faculty who are committed to the mission, but they also support opportunities for faculty to grow in their understanding and expression of the mission. In decisions regarding academic budgeting and planning, the board ensures that funding and systems are in place for appropriate faculty development, research, and curriculum design, the vibrant heart of the institution. The mission officer can bring very helpful and specific recommendations to the board throughout this process.

The mission officer at NDMU has been the inspiration behind Community Day, with a focus on Catholic Social Teaching, and lends guidance to Notre Dame Day, a tradition whose roots date to the early 1900s, with the goal of educating the student body about the university mission in action. Both annual events are planned by committees of faculty and staff.

The board of trustees will especially want to know how the mission is communicated to new faculty and staff members. At NDMU, the mission officer grounds their orientation in the belief that all university community members are "Partners in Mission," the theme of the annual recognition event celebrating faculty and staff years of service. Some of the most effective initiatives informed by this philosophy include a six-part program for new vice presidents, a yearlong seminar for new faculty, and a process for intentional recruiting of faculty and staff known as "Hiring for Mission," which helps prepare candidates to know and understand the importance of mission. In an even broader context, the

Acknowledging a decrease in the number of sisters in active ministry, the mission officer helped plan and direct a two-day off-site retreat for all trustees with other School Sisters of Notre Dame. The program explored seamless connections between the SSND charism and the NDMU mission, and it highlighted the trustees' role in carrying forward the mantle of SSND legacy.

mission officer is both responsive to requests for presentations on mission and proactive in capturing new opportunities to integrate the mission message into special events on campus. In partnership with the president, the mission officer can assure the board that the goal of each outreach activity is to build up a university committed to the mission, which is their charge as trustees.

## Collaboration with the Congregational Mission Officer

Since most Catholic colleges and universities were founded by religious congregations, it is essential that the mission officer effectively connect the vision of the founding community with the leadership of the higher education community. While this can be complex, it can also be immensely fruitful. The congregation's mission informs and directs its sponsorship of the college or university, and its own representatives on the board must ensure that trustees recognize and reflect the congregational mission as inspiration and foundation for the university's mission. The two mission statements, one of the sponsoring congregation and one of the university, are complementary, but their purposes remain distinct. The congregation's mission officers, whether religious or lay, work closely with the board in parallel with the university's mission officer. Building a strong mutual relationship, together they educate and guide trustees in understanding the sponsors' mission and the ways it informs the mission of the institution.

## Full Partnership in Mission Messaging

The goal of every mission officer is, in ways particular to his or her institution, exactly that—to bring all community members into full partnership in mission messaging, so that the decisions they make, the programs they design, the curricula they teach, and the lives they lead at the university make its mission concrete. A strong relationship with the board of trustees extends the mission officer's circle of effective communication. When the board, the president, and the mission officer are fully and mutually engaged in the effort, the mission message is communicated deeply and broadly, across campus and beyond, from the present into the future.

*Donna Easton is Trustee, Vice-Chair of the Academic Affairs Committee of the Board of Trustees, and an alumna of Notre Dame of Maryland University, Baltimore, MD.*

*Sr. Christine De Vinne, OSU is Vice President for Academic Affairs at Notre Dame of Maryland University, Baltimore, MD.*

## section FOUR
● ● ● ● ● ●

**Charism and Mission**

## chapter EIGHTEEN

## Charism as the Primary Door into the Catholic Mission

*Sean Peters, CSJ*

In Catholic tradition, a charism is a special gift given by the Spirit of God to a group for the good of the Church and the world. Each religious congregation possesses a particular charism which forms the core of their special gift to the Church. Charisms are deep, multidimensional, spiritual gifts, often better experienced than explained; but the concept of charism has been present since the earliest days of the Church. For example, each of the four Gospels emphasizes a different dimension of Jesus' life—in a sense a different charism manifested by Jesus. Paul, too, reminds us that there are different gifts, but the same Spirit is manifested through all of them (1 Corinthians 12:4).

A few examples may help the reader to better understand the meaning of charism in religious congregations. The Sisters of St. Joseph describe their charism as "active, inclusive love" or as a constant movement toward "unity and reconciliation." The Religious Sisters of Mercy seek to incarnate the Mercy of God to the poor, sick, and ignorant. The Dominican charism can be expressed as the desire to "share with others the truth about the God whom we contemplate in our hearts." While these brief expressions fall far short in describing the rich gifts of the Spirit given to each congregation for the good of the Church, they do attempt to show how various religious congregations have, at their core, a focus on different aspects of the Gospel message.

While an institution of higher education has a distinct mission from that of a religious congregation, the mission of the college or university certainly reflects that of the founding congregation. So, for example, the Conference of Mercy Higher Education website indicates that the ministry of higher education "expresses our commitment … to the furtherance of the social, political, economic, and spiritual wellbeing of the human community." Dominican University states as part of its mission that it "prepares students to pursue truth." Avila University, founded by the Sisters of St. Joseph, says that it is "a values-based *community* of learning." With these few examples, one can see that the core values of the founding congregation find their way into the contemporary expression of the institution's mission.

To function effectively, the mission officer must immerse himself or herself in the values of the founding charism. While, those mission officers who are members of the founding community have the benefit of religious formation and a lifetime of exploring and living these values, all mission officers have the responsibility to understand the

Inculcating the charism often does not mean doing more things, but rather doing the same differently. For example, in introducing this guest speaker at the College of Saint Rose, the topic was connected to the charism: "We have invited Dr. X to be with us today because his writings reflect so clearly his commitment to inclusive community, one of the core values of our founders, the Sisters of Saint Joseph."

• • • • • • • • • • • • • • • • • • • • • • • • • • • • • • • •

nuances of the charism as it applies to higher education and to continue to develop their understanding of how the charism can be lived out in the contemporary world. Mission officers who take the time to reflect on these values will find a rich source for their conversations and programming. Catholic universities and religious communities that invest time and money in the education and formation of their senior administrators help to ensure a connection with the founding charism and the heartbeat of the academic enterprise of a Catholic university.

At many institutions today, talk of Catholic identity or even the Catholic Intellectual Tradition can turn contentious quite quickly, but usually the values of the founding charism are held in common esteem. For some, the word *Catholic* elicits an image of a cold, misdirected institutional church, while the words associated with a charism elicit a desirable value advancing the common good. These life-giving values of the charism are almost "in the air" of most institutions. They are accepted as normative and ordinary. Rather than dividing the community, they tend to unite different factions around commonly held values. A successful mission officer helps the university community recognize that the highly esteemed virtues of the founding charism emerged from the Judeo-Christian story, and the charism is embedded within the Catholic family of virtues.

When the mission officer helps the community understand the connection between charism and the Catholic faith, it is easier to match these institutional core values with the values that underlie the Catholic Intellectual Tradition. The Catholic Intellectual Tradition, when seen as 2,000 years of wise advice on how to advance the common good, can become a repository of wisdom on which to build an authentic, healthy life today. The mission officer who can assist faculty and staff in developing a process that helps students discover intelligent and clever insights from Catholic sages of yesteryear advances the best thinking of today with a

At the College of Saint Rose, the faculty/staff orientation for new employees begins with the history and stories of the Sisters of Saint Joseph. Their four core values are enumerated and detailed. Then the various ways these values reflect the values of the Catholic Intellectual Tradition (CIT) are demonstrated. We were not successful during a previous year when we began with the values of the CIT and followed them with the core values of the charism.

• • • • • • • • • • • • • • • • • • • • • • • • • • • • • • • •

rich intellectual tradition grounded in authenticity and the good life. It is little wonder that those who began religious communities were attracted to a life where certain values and virtues were seen as life-giving and simultaneously provided enlightening solutions to contemporary challenges. Put in this light, it makes sense that the charism values and the principles of the Catholic Intellectual Tradition overlap with the Catholic worldview based on the teachings of Jesus. It will be essential for the mission officer to create educational and conversational opportunities where these important connections can be discovered.

Once this is begun, the mission officer can use the widely accepted charism values as a door into the discussions and programming of Catholic identity. In a real way, the charism provides a common lens with which the campus community can view the philosophies that underlie Catholic higher education. Of course, first the mission officer must make certain that, if the campus community has not already done so, the values of the charism are highlighted, agreed upon, and even celebrated.

The Sisters of Saint Joseph value service to neighbors (where all are neighbors and each one dear). This is celebrated during Heritage Week when the Heritage and Mission Committee highlights the number of volunteer hours that students, faculty, and staff offered to the wider community, the number of different organizations served, and the number of courses that include service-learning. These facts are printed and displayed around campus and also sent as e-mails to the community.

Once these charism values become part of common conversation, they can guide decision-making matrices, strategic planning processes, and form the base for curricular decisions, student programming, and marketing strategies. If those who guide the institution continue to underscore the unity between these core values and the Catholic Intellectual Tradition, this can lead to a more comfortable acceptance of the Catholic identity of the institution by all stakeholders in the organization.

Alternatively, if the mission officer does not keep the values of the founding charism before the eyes of both the campus community and its wider publics, the power of these values can quickly dissipate. American higher education is replete with examples of this phenomenon in former faith-based institutions. While these institutions may still have fine educational practices, they have lost the power provided by a campus-wide commitment to commonly held values which are also strongly supported and enhanced by groups outside the university (with Catholic institutions this would be their founding congregation and the Catholic Church). Perhaps the greatest loss for these formerly faith-based institutions is the rich interaction which comes from the interplay between faith and reason. Further, failure to educate the spiritual dimension of students may truncate the education of the whole person emphasized in the Catholic Intellectual Tradition.

Wise mission officers, then, continue to deepen their understanding of the charism of the founding congregation, reflect on its application to the needs of the contemporary world, and do all they can to integrate these values into all aspects of the campus community. If they do this, they will find in these values a powerfully unifying and energizing resource for the institution.

*Sr. Sean Peters, CSJ is Director of Mission Experience at The College of Saint Rose, Albany, NY.*

## chapter NINETEEN

## A Sacred Trust: The Mission Officer and the Sponsoring Congregation

*Kathleen Cornell, SSND*

On college and university campuses where there is a sponsoring religious congregation, the sponsoring charism is a special way of shaping the response to God's call in the Church and for the world.

The charism of the School Sisters of Notre Dame (SSND) is embodied in their efforts to bring about unity, belief in community, ministries focused on education, and common search for God's will.

●●●●●●●●●●●●●●●●●●●●●●●●●●●●●●●●●

The religious congregation shares the gift of its sacred trust and typically is an integral component of the institution. In turn, the institution's leadership, mission office, and community receive and share the gift in a manner that ensures the charism is embodied in vibrant and lasting ways. Efforts of the mission officer are reflective of the values and principles of the religious congregation as well as the universal Church; when they are fully embraced, they foster the life of the members of the university community, especially when the mission office makes necessary links to articulate their relevance to today. In short, the institution not only understands, but radiates the mission and charism of its sponsoring congregation.

This chapter will explore how the sacred trust of the congregation is shared and ways the mission officer can foster that sacred trust within the institution. If a strong relationship between the religious congregation and the university does not already exist, the mission officer is called upon to develop this essential relationship.

### Sacred Trust

Religious congregations involved in higher education place the mission and charism of their community into the competent hands and devoted hearts of university leadership. Although senior leadership and mission officers are typically well-equipped to uphold the trust of the congregation, it is helpful when the religious congregation provides ongoing ministry and spiritual formation for both the president and the chair of the board, as well as other senior administrators including the mission officer.

The mission officer, in conjunction with the religious congregational leadership and the university senior leadership, honors this sacred trust through agreement upon rituals and practices honoring the relationship and agreement on assessment tools that ascertain the charism's vibrancy at the institution. For instance, rituals for Foundation Day or anniversaries of service celebrations should have a congregational emphasis focusing on the congregation's charism and legacy. Another excellent opportunity is the installation of a new president, during which time he or she can publicly articulate the importance of the congregation's presence. Understanding the importance of assessment, one institution identified four defining characteristics of its sponsored works. Then an assessment process was developed in which the institution described ways these characteristics were manifested.

When agreeing to carry on the tradition of the sponsoring religious congregation, the college or university accepts the responsibility to continue the work of God grounded in the mission and charism of the particular tradition. In collaboration with and supported by the president, the mission officer is a leader in building a culture where the charism of the religious congregation is visible and transformative. Development of a comprehensive, ongoing program of education for the institution's community is a lasting way to build this culture.

For example, the mission officer's work with the board and president to raise the level of their awareness and commitment to the charism and mission is a fundamental way to create common knowledge, understanding, and appreciation of the unique gifts, traditions, and practices of a particular congregation. It is also beneficial when the president and the congregational leader work well together. This is especially true if the congregational leaders are those canonically responsible for the institution. In some congregations, there is a mission effectiveness office that acts as a link between the congregation and the ministries. This role can be helpful to the mission officer by providing concrete and tested ways in which mission can be actualized.

## Mission Effectiveness Office

Mission officers, in collaboration with others, take the lead in responding intentionally to continue God's work in the university. Depending on the background of the mission officer, the first step in advancing mission may be to learn about the congregation and the university. The mission officer needs to know the history and be familiar with the constitution of the congregation, talk to sisters, brothers, and priests about the congregation, and ascertain the level of understanding of the mission of the congregation by the university community. This can be done by talking with faculty, staff, board members, and student leaders in addition to reading the mission statement and reviewing the strategic

The Sisters of St. Joseph of Carondelet share their charism's heritage with faculty, staff, students, and the local community at Fontebonne University through lunch-time presentations and conversations. Other groups join in; for example, the Social Work Student Association co-sponsored a sister working with traumatized refugees.

plan, the website, and publications. Mission officers are essential, but they cannot be solely responsible for this ministry. The president, vice presidents, deans, chairs, administrators, and other leaders are partners. All members of the university community should be involved in the endeavors of the mission office.

The primary responsibility of the mission officer is to create a culture grounded in the sacred trust given to that higher education institution. This means being an advocate for building relationships, developing program curricula, and creating rituals and mission-centered environments. Thus, the mission officer encourages relationships between leadership of the congregation and the university, develops relationships with members of the religious congregation on campus and at the headquarters of the congregation, and visits with sisters, brothers, and priests in retirement residences and other ministries. He or she arranges for invitations to congregational leaders, sisters, brothers, and priests to be present on campus and to participate as appropriate in major events. If the congregation has meetings or retreats, the mission officer attends them and encourages others to attend as appropriate.

In particular, the mission officer has an important role in having a seat at the table during institution-wide strategic decisions. While each college or university is at a different stage of developing comprehensive programs for their university communities, the mission officer should be involved in these significant mission activities: creating human resource guidelines for hiring; developing orientation programs; planning celebrations grounded in mission; influencing the campus environment and participating in the design of sacred spaces so as to reflect the charism through art and architecture; honoring and retelling the congregation's story; and coordinating ongoing educational opportunities.

**Conclusion**

The congregation as sponsor, and the president and the board, must determine how mission is being advanced on campus. The mission officer designs and implements the plan. Establishing a way to examine and verify mission effectiveness helps to affirm the sacred trust and to identify areas of growth. Some congregations have a process for reviewing the work and life of the university. They access how well the mission and charism are being lived and what needs to be done to further God's mission. The mission officer is a leader within the living university community in the unfolding of God's mission for the life of the world.

"Charism continues to develop in the living community, which, enriched by the past, enables the congregation [and university] to unfold in the present and to be challenged by the future." (School Sisters of Notre Dame, 1986)

*Sr. Kathleen Cornell, SSND is Provincial Leader, School Sisters of Notre Dame, Atlantic-Midwest Province, Baltimore, MD.*

*Reference*
School Sisters of Notre Dame. (1986). *You Are Sent: Constitution and General Directory.* Milwaukee, WI.

## chapter TWENTY

## The Religious Charism of a University and Its Catholic Character: A Jesuit Way of Proceeding

*Kevin O'Brien, SJ*

The mission statement of Georgetown University begins, "Georgetown is a Catholic and Jesuit, student-centered research university." A close reading of this simple, declarative statement reveals some underlying tension: between student-centered and research, for example, and among Catholic, Jesuit, and university. The Catholic imagination, however, strives to reconcile apparent tensions into a coherent whole, avoiding facile "either/or" contrasts and embracing "both/and" possibilities. The human and the divine, the secular and the sacred, nature and grace, and faith and reason are paired sides of a single coin, complementary ways of experiencing the one and same Holy Mystery. Thus, while some may find the university's Catholic character, its religious charism (Jesuit), and its academic mission as inherently at odds, one with a Catholic imagination sees connection. Though the mix of Catholic, charism, and university is challenging at times, Catholic higher education is at its best in the competitive world of higher education when it authentically expresses itself. A Catholic university thrives when it does not diminish the underlying tension inherent in its mission, but embraces it as a creative moment, filled with promise and opportunity.

> "There are three extraordinary resources that we bring to bear on our choices about how best to realize our Catholic and Jesuit identity …: First, the Catholic Intellectual Tradition; second, our Jesuit heritage … and third, our understanding of the fundamental importance of tradition." (President DeGioia, Georgetown University, June 2012)

Any Catholic university is first of all a university. God has given each person the capacity to discover truth, create knowledge, revel in beauty, and grow in goodness. At a university, faculty and students alike are privileged to pursue these opportunities in a conversation with one another and with great thinkers and artists across the ages. At a Catholic university, those within the university appreciate that the Spirit of God inspires and guides these conversations. Such inspiration and guidance, by Catholic reckoning, in no way inhibits genuine human freedom, but fosters it, and allows everyone to flourish as human persons.

The Catholic Church has long relied on the university to ferment a healthy exchange between faith and reason. Augustine, Anselm, and other great thinkers instruct those willing to listen that faith always seeks understanding. Because God is the ground of all reality, nothing is outside the realm of investigation—whether in the liberal arts, the sciences, or the professions of law, medicine, and business. For the inquisitive seeker, the "sacred" reveals itself in the "ordinary." The more one knows, the more God is revealed. Catholic tradition, properly understood, does not threaten the pursuit of academic excellence, but only deepens it, bringing two thousand years of accumulated wisdom, inquiry, and values to the conversation.

> "In promoting the integration of knowledge, a specific part of a Catholic University's task is to promote dialogue between faith and reason, so that it can be seen more profoundly how faith and reason bear harmonious witness to the unity of all truth." (Pope John Paul II, *Ex corde Ecclesiae,* 17)

Mindful of this Spirit-inspired freedom within the context of a university, it is axiomatic that our common inquiry must be unfettered. No question is off-limits, and no well-intended speculation out of bounds. Through the crucible of rigorous scholarly exchange, all proposals and hypotheses are tested. In seeking after the good, the true, and the beautiful, ideas are inevitably encountered which are eccentric, offensive, or even repulsive. At a Catholic university, no less than any other university, confidence abounds that scholarly conversation intrinsic to our community can effectively sort through the wheat and chaff of ideas and leave the latter to their own decomposition.

> "As a Jesuit university, we are called to be at the frontiers—and our work in academic excellence, in extending the spiritual resources of our tradition into the life of our community, in deepening our capacity to promote interreligious understanding, in living out our responsibility to address issues of social justice, and in sustaining our engagement with our culture—are examples of our effort to deepen our tradition." (President DeGioia, Georgetown University, June 2012)

A Catholic university is called to foster a critical conversation about ideas and issues at the intersection of faith and culture. While permitting expression that sometimes challenges the Church's view of reality, the Catholic university can give eloquent voice to the Catholic intellectual, artistic, and moral tradition in a number of ways, among them: undergraduate theology and philosophy requirements in the core curriculum; a cross-curricular Catholic Studies program; a vibrant campus ministry with an array of liturgies, retreats, and faith formation programs; the collaborative work of colleagues in student development and residential life; co-curricular student dialogues on contemporary issues in the Church and society; social justice and service programs; and finally, the vital engagement of a sponsoring religious community. A mission officer's chief role is to foster connections among these various parts of the university community, so that everyone is invested in the university's religious identity.

The charism of a university adds a distinctive accent to this conversation among friends and scholars and often can serve as the bridge across differences. Throughout the

Church's history, religious orders emerged to help the Church think, teach, pray, and serve differently so as to meet emerging and unmet needs. The Second Vatican Council called on religious orders to embrace their unique charism and interpret it in ways both faithful to their tradition and meaningful for people in the modern world. As a place where talented men and women from all walks of life gather, the Catholic university is an ideal setting where a charism can rediscover its roots and find creative expression.

"What differentiates a Catholic and Jesuit university is the privilege given to a specific tradition: the tradition given to us at the time of our founding, the tradition which is at the center of our identity. While we will defend and sustain a plurality of perspectives at the university, we prioritize the one that has animated this community for more than two centuries." (President DeGioia, Georgetown University, June 2012)

The university's mission office must collaborate with the founding religious community to share that charism in engaging ways through scholarly presentation, spiritual programs, and service opportunities. Not to be underestimated, however, is the significant impact that informal social gatherings have on a campus culture. At Georgetown, for example, the Jesuit community hosts new faculty at the beginning of the academic year and later welcomes staff and faculty for a Christmas party. Such relationship-building is particularly important for those who are not familiar with the charism or who do not share Catholic religious commitments. These social gatherings often help begin conversations and relationships that eventually lead to more intentional discussion and appreciation for the university's religious charism. The Georgetown Jesuit Community has dedicated space in its building to host faculty, staff, and students who are making various retreats based on the Spiritual Exercises of St. Ignatius, the founder of the Jesuits. Friendship, usually cultivated over many semesters, is often the most fertile ground for learning and creative collaboration for mission.

To be successful, this mission-promotion work depends on the participation and presence of priests and religious brothers and sisters formed in the charism. At the same time, often the most eloquent and effective presenters of a charism are lay people who are

"We are living in an age when the spirituality of St. Ignatius of Loyola is more accessible than at virtually any time in modern history." (President DeGioia, Georgetown University, June 2012)

steeped in the tradition and who can translate it to a largely lay audience of students, faculty, staff, and alumni.

In facilitating the conversation about what it means to be a Catholic university grounded in a particular charism, two inclinations must be avoided. The first is to pit the Catholic against the charism. Some at the university may view the religious community as diluting the university's Catholic character; others who struggle with the institutional Church or particular teachings may proudly claim the charism while disavowing the Catholic. While it is important to understand where these voices are coming from, the mission office must call everyone back to the "both/and." A charism cannot be separated from the Church and is always in service of the Church; yet, sometimes that service is best offered, as in the prophetic tradition, by raising provocative questions and challenging perspectives.

The second inclination to avoid is competitiveness among institutions. Georgetown, for example, is part of a larger family of twenty-eight Jesuit colleges and universities and over two hundred Catholic institutions of higher learning in the United States. While the leaders at each school are aware of the various rankings and compete in similar pools for the best professors and students, healthy competition must not undermine opportunities for greater collaboration. Like different religious orders, each Catholic college or university offers the Church and the world something distinctive. That unique contribution must be recognized and leveraged.

"Our Catholic Intellectual Tradition is an extraordinary strategic advantage … a gift that we will protect and strengthen now, and into the future." (President DeGioia, Georgetown University, June 2012)

By working more closely together—bilaterally and collectively—Catholic higher education can ensure that meaningful leadership continues amid the increasingly complex realities of higher education. The Catholic tradition has something to offer the academy through our centuries-old commitment to bridging faith and reason and to forming men and women of compassion and conviction. That vital voice will best be heard if it speaks in chorus.

God is at work on each and every campus: this is the underlying presumption of those engaged in Catholic higher education. Thus, each university is more than a collection of bright minds and beautiful buildings. Each Catholic university has a soul, a spirit that emanates from its Catholic tradition and, for many, its distinctive religious charism. The mission officer is privileged to lead and enable the community in bringing the Catholic, the charism, and the university into a spirited conversation to serve the greater glory of God.

*Rev. Kevin O'Brien, SJ is Vice President for Mission and Ministry at Georgetown University, Washington, DC.*

*Reference*

DeGioia, J. (2012, June). *Where the World Meets the Church and the Church Meets the World.* Speech presented at Georgetown University, Georgetown, DC.

## chapter TWENTY-ONE

## Compassion and Diversity: Integrating the Mercy Charism in the Mission Office

*Leona Misto, RSM*

The values of harmony, justice, and mercy are at the heart of the Mercy Tradition. Created in God's image, all people deserve respect, hospitality, and compassion. Working for social justice begins by not merely accepting, but welcoming people of all faiths. By embracing diversity, people of good will acknowledge the universal call to be a steward of creation, and to care for and live in harmony with one another as well as the environment. At Salve Regina University these values of the Mercy Tradition are put into practice in a variety of ways.

During the early years of the college, the Sisters of Mercy who taught and administered gave witness to the values and the history of Salve Regina. In these times, it is necessary to remind, or in many cases inform, persons of the sustaining values of the sisters and the history of the university. To this end, a video interview with sisters who ministered during the early years conveys their thoughts about the culture of the university, the customs of the students, and the founding spirit of the Sisters of Mercy. The video, "The Early Years," truly captures the essence of those years and is used in various ways by individuals on campus. It can be viewed at http://salve.edu/ under the "Mission" heading. Campus buildings that were named in honor of particular sisters have photos of the sisters on display and plaques describing their contributions.

The booklet, *Salve Regina University's Story: The Heritage and the Promise*, captures the essence of the vision of the founding sisters and informs persons about the current position of the university and its promise of continued development. The booklet is distributed to new members of the university community as well as to parents of incoming students.

More recently, the University Mission Committee initiated a university-wide discussion on the virtue of *mercy*; specifically, how the Mercy charism relates to and is integrated into the curriculum. This project engaged faculty in discovering ways to integrate mercy into the curriculum by analyzing the meaning of mercy in a particular discipline. The first case study addressed by faculty from Science, Business Studies, and Religious and Theological Studies focused on Hurricane Katrina. The science faculty focused on the suffering caused by contaminated water, infections, and disease. They designed ways to form teams to help address these issues. Business faculty were appalled by the chaos resulting from deficient management and coordination of the relief efforts. They too suggested ways to address the identified concerns. As one might expect, the Religious Studies faculty were concerned with the spiritual and personal welfare of the victims. Their goal was to provide assistance in finding relatives, connecting with family, and trying to locate lost pets.

Many signs of Mercy traditions are found on campus. Granite stones engraved with pertinent sayings of Catherine McAuley, foundress of the Sisters of Mercy, have been placed at strategic locations. One entering the dining hall reads, "Try to meet all with peace and ease." Posters identifying the Corporal and Spiritual Works of Mercy are displayed in buildings throughout the campus. Bookmarks of the Works of Mercy are distributed to all newcomers.

During the course of this project, twenty-nine faculty representing thirteen academic departments participated in creating a model for inter-departmental conversations about mercy and means of integrating mercy into the curriculum. The final year of this project concluded with a university-wide symposium, *Mercy Illuminates*, at which eight faculty members presented papers on the virtue of mercy. The papers addressed topics related to the Meaning of Mercy, Justice, Mercy and the State, and service-learning. The papers were published and widely distributed and can be found at http://escholar.salve.edu/mercy/.

## Integrating Diversity

The world has become smaller and more diverse. Respect and acceptance of all people is a fundamental component of Mercy's Catholic mission. All parts of society must be validated and incorporated to function as a whole. That same integration of nations and cultures is reflected in the Mercy charism of diversity and hospitality. The concerted effort at Salve Regina to assist faculty, staff, and students in promoting diversity through university-wide programs and projects demonstrates integration of this Mercy charism.

A ten-minute mission video highlights faculty, staff, and students who share their thoughts on various aspects of the university mission that distinguish Salve Regina from other Catholic universities. This video is shown during student orientations and campus tours.

Early on, the Mission Integration Office partnered with the National Conference of Community and Justice to offer training sessions to faculty and staff on discrimination and racial injustice. One result of this effort was the establishment of a line item in the university budget to offer financial assistance to minority students from diverse backgrounds and cultures. As a result, the number of minority students entering the university increased from 4.3 percent in 2001 to 14.7 percent in 2011.

Once scholarships were available, it became evident that the economically disadvantaged students who received tuition needed additional assistance with books and other materials necessary to complete their education. The Vice President for Mission Integration obtained funding through grants and used the money to assist students, particularly women, with aid for textbooks, supplies, daycare, and nursing equipment. Since beginning this work, the Mission Office has received over $114,000, and a revolving textbook fund is in place to help students. One hundred forty-four grants have been awarded to students since this program was initiated.

The vice president also chaired the University Multicultural Committee, which was established to help retain students from diverse backgrounds. The committee sponsored numerous events on campus to celebrate cultural heritages. In the fall, local Hispanic artists were invited to display their works and Native Americans were guest speakers. In the spring, programs for Black Heritage Month and Women's Month were held.

A team of faculty worked with the vice president to create a Diversity Dialogue Forum, which provided faculty from different departments an opportunity to exchange ideas on integrating diversity into the curricular. Faculty met twice each semester to discuss topics related to creating an inclusive classroom, teaching for diversity, managing diversity in the classroom, and identifying curriculum issues that should be included in the syllabus. During a period of three years, forty faculty from fifteen disciplines participated in the dialogue. These efforts led to the creation and hiring of a Director of Multicultural Programs.

The Church's emphasis and continuing work toward social justice demonstrates the value and necessity of diversity in creating a world in which people and creation thrive. The Mercy charisms of respect and acceptance, shown through the various ways the Salve Regina community chooses to integrate diversity at their university, are the embodiment of the Church's mission.

> The Faces of Mercy Contest is an annual event that invites faculty, staff, and students to submit a photo, drawing, narrative, poem, or a visual depicting mercy in action at the university. Marketing students administer the contest, design flyers, and promote the event. Recently, among thirty-four entries, first place went to a student who entered a photo of her four-year-old brother making a wish for his grandmother to be cured of cancer, while he shared his birthday cake with her in the nursing home.

*Sr. Leona Misto, RSM is Vice President for Mission Integration at Salve Regina University, Newport, RI.*

## chapter TWENTY-TWO

## What Makes a Sponsorship Agreement and How to Create One

*Sean C. Peters, CSJ*
*Gloria Urrabazo*

A mission officer needs to know four things about sponsorship as it relates to the university and the founding congregation. The first is how sponsorship is defined and understood. The second is how the stakeholders understand the relationship between the sponsoring congregation and the university. The definition of the term "sponsorship" needs to be clearly understood by all constituents such as the board of trustees, administration, faculty, staff, and alumni. The third is the importance of the role that the mission officer plays in implementing the agreement. The fourth is how to create a sponsorship agreement which can enhance understanding between the congregation and the university.

### What Does Sponsorship Mean?

It is well known what sponsorship means when used regarding a company like General Electric; but, what does it mean when applied to an organization associated with the Catholic Intellectual Tradition? The word *sponsorship* entered the vocabulary of Catholic institutions about thirty years ago, as the number of people from the founding congregations started to significantly decline at various Catholic entities. The word *sponsorship* is not found in the Code of Canon Law, and the Church does not define it in other Church documents. Sponsorship is a term used in North America to describe the ever-evolving relationship between religious institutes and the institutions which they founded and, for many years, owned, administered, managed, and staffed. It is the purpose of a sponsorship document to clarify and articulate the meaning and the implications of the relationship between the university and its founder.

Fundamentally, the university derives its Catholic identity from its affiliation with its sponsoring congregation. Codified by an agreement between the organization and the founding congregation, sponsorship of any entity is a board-to-board, mission-to-mission relationship. The board of trustees and the congregational leadership team make an agreement (usually a formal agreement, but sometimes informal) with the board of the sponsored entity. While the mission of the sponsored institution differs from the mission of the sponsoring congregation, one will see echoes of the sponsoring congregation in the mission of the university. While both the congregation and the university may have a commitment to service, the distinct purpose of the two organizations would mean that each would do this differently. The congregation might encourage direct service and advocacy for those in need. The university, on the other hand, might use service-learning as pedagogy to assist its students to learn various values or content material through their service experience. Both are committed to service, but the way they live out that value differs because the purposes of the organizations differ.

Each party of the sponsorship agreement has particular benefits and responsibilities. For example, in terms of responsibilities, the sponsoring congregation often reserves some powers, such as the right to appoint the president of the institution or to appoint persons to a certain number of seats on the board of the university. The college, for its part, agrees to keep the Catholic founding values alive on campus and indicates its willingness to demonstrate and evaluate how those values are implemented.

## How Sponsorship Is Understood on a Given Campus

Since there is no clear definition of sponsorship, the term in any given institution is defined by its own agreement with the congregation and the sponsoring institution. The responsibility of the mission officer is to study, implement, and evaluate programs that enhance the relationship between the congregation and the university.

If there is no document, but there does exist some "understanding" between the parties, the mission officer might consider the benefit of suggesting something more formal to ensure a continued collaboration between the sponsoring congregation and the college or university. It is strongly encouraged that a sponsorship agreement be drawn up. It will not only protect both constituents but will also uphold the Catholic identity of the institution. It will also strengthen the religious heritage of the founding congregation. Otherwise, as board members on both sides of the equation change, the understanding might become less clear or even cause contention between the two groups. While a written agreement does not preclude disagreement, it can help to avoid assumptions and misunderstandings between the two boards and other affected parties.

## The Responsibilities of the Mission Officer

In addition to studying and understanding the sponsorship agreement, the mission officer can assist the president in his or her fulfillment of the agreement. For example, many sponsorship agreements call for a periodic conversation between the two parties in which the institution indicates how it has fulfilled the agreement and embodied the core values of the institution. The mission officer, aware of these periodic reports, can fashion assessments that will ensure that the appropriate data are available when reports are requested. Assessments are created out of the goals and objectives of the sponsorship agreement.

Of course, the mission officer's primary responsibility to the sponsorship agreement is assuring that the core values of the mission find themselves infused in all aspects of institutional life. This is the true purpose of the mission agreement—that the mission of the institution embodies and spreads the core values of the sponsoring congregation.

If mission officers know the key elements of the sponsorship agreement, plan for its implementation, and do all they can to make sure that the mission of the institution penetrates all aspects of the university, any sponsorship agreement will be well fulfilled.

### Creating a Sponsorship Agreement

In a sponsorship agreement, the relationship between the sponsor and the sponsored institution is laid out, and the attendant benefits and responsibilities of each party are described. It is important to consider what the college or university offers the sponsor and what the sponsor can provide to the institution. Founders and the sponsored institution bind themselves in this covenant to grow in understanding and practice of mutual commitment to shared values, vision, and mission.

Usually, the sponsor gains an extension of the mission of the congregation, especially through the opportunity to educate more people about the congregation's charism. In return, the sponsor accepts the responsibility to educate key people in the charism in an ongoing manner.

The college or university, for its part, benefits from the good name and reputation of the congregation, and the charism education provided by the sponsor strengthens the institution's mission integration. The institution takes responsibility for encouraging faculty and staff to deepen their appreciation of the values of the founding congregation, to participate in charism education, and to share with the congregation an assessment of how the campus community embodies the values of the founding congregation.

A step-by-step process for creating a sponsorship agreement might include:

- Identify the key players in the institution. Do not go forward without the expressed agreement of the president or chancellor of the institution. Be sure faculty are included.
- Identify some potential benefits and responsibilities of the sponsorship partners.
- Gather people from the congregational leadership and the institution's board to help prepare materials for their respective boards. This helps to model the collaboration the sponsorship agreement is designed to foster and institutionalize.
- Discuss the model of sponsorship that will be initiated. For example, some institutions have a shared philosophy of sponsorship while others draw up a binding legal document.
- Draft a sponsorship agreement and submit it to the two parties for action. (An easy way to complete this step is to identify institutions similar in size and character to one's institution and solicit their sponsorship agreements. This can provide models that can assist in developing an agreement.)
- If the agreement is adopted, celebrate appropriately.
- Structures need to be put in place that will support the agreement. For example, in collaboration with the congregation, design the charism education plan. Set up the values assessment procedures.
- The agreement must be concise and reviewed with the college community and the board every year.

In summary, the sponsorship agreement ensures the ongoing relevance of the sponsoring congregation's charism and provides the university with clear direction and purpose of their role in the living legacy of the founding congregation. It is the role of the mission officer to keep before the university's leadership the importance of the document and provide programs that will embody the mission.

*Sr. Sean Peters, CSJ is Director of Mission Experience at The College of Saint Rose, Albany, NY.*

*Gloria Urrabazo is Vice President for Mission and Ministry at Our Lady of the Lake University, San Antonio, TX.*

## chapter TWENTY-THREE

## Sponsorship Covenants and Mission Officers: A Case in Point

*Thomas F. Flynn*
*Roberta A. McKelvie, OSF*

During 2012–2013, the Board of Trustees of Alvernia University (PA) and the school's sponsoring religious congregation, the Bernardine Franciscan Sisters, took historic actions to strengthen an already strong relationship. They adopted both a first-ever Sponsorship Covenant and a revised set of Reserved Powers, the results of a three-year process of study, reflection, and dialogue by a Sponsorship Learning Community (SLC). At the same time, implementation began of a comprehensive mission education and integration program, drafted by a Franciscan Learning Community (FLC) comprised of faculty, staff, administrators, and sisters from the sponsoring congregation. Taken together, this work culminated a multi-year strategic focus on Alvernia's mission and identity, launched by the new president in 2006 and codified by the strategic plan (2007, 2012). It also serves as a case study of the pivotal and evolving role of the mission officer, the centrality of mission-centered presidential leadership, and the multiple partnerships necessary for a genuine institutional commitment to mission.

### Background and Context

A Franciscan university of 3,000 students, Alvernia University is designated by the Carnegie Foundation as a national model of community and civic engagement. When the new president arrived in 2005, several members of the religious congregation served not only in part-time positions, but also as trustees. A Franciscan sister served as Vice President for Mission and Ministry and as a member of the president's cabinet. Her major responsibilities were to supervise campus ministry, interview potential faculty and staff candidates, lead an annual Mission Day program, and promote appreciation for the mission.

"Mission and Identity" discussions hosted by the new president revealed strong respect for the school's Franciscan heritage

New vision and mission statements, drafted to frame the 2007 strategic plan, articulated both the aspiration to be a "distinctive Franciscan university" rooted in the Catholic and liberal arts traditions, and the commitment to Alvernia's five Franciscan core values: collegiality, contemplation, humility, peacemaking, and service.

•••••••••••••••••••••••••••••••••••

and values, though most equated that identity solely with the "ministry of presence" by the sisters and the campus' devotion to community service. The widespread practice of the Mission Moment—a brief time of reflection at the opening of campus events, meetings, and classes—indicated a readiness for deeper learning about and reflection on the Franciscan, Catholic character of the institution.

The first of the plan's five priorities focused on becoming a mission-centered university with a stronger commitment to Franciscan identity. As part of a comprehensive review of the role of the mission office, the president and the current mission vice president agreed to reassign campus ministry to the University Life division. In this way, campus ministry could more effectively facilitate collaborations with other dimensions of student life and enhance mission education efforts. Following an interim period and consultations with fellow presidents, as well as campus and congregational leaders, the president redefined the nature of the mission officer position and created the cabinet-level position of Special Assistant to the President for Mission Integration and Education.

### The Franciscan Learning Community (FLC)

The most dramatic mission-centered initiative was the creation of a presidentially appointed Franciscan Learning Community (FLC). A collection of faculty, staff, students, and congregational leaders, it was charged to engage in a two-year "process of discernment, planning, and action about mission and identity" that would lead to the "design of a robust program of mission education for the university community." Led by the interim mission officer, a Mercy sister from the faculty with significant leadership experience, this learning community moved through a series of retreats, readings, study, discussion, and engagement with distinguished scholars. Members read and reflected on the Catholic and Franciscan intellectual traditions, the history and heritage of the Bernardine Franciscan Sisters, and the core values and principles of Alvernia University. This learning community became a "seed group" for expanding institutional understanding of the university's identity and mission.

The 2010 final report of the FLC contained a lengthy statement of "shared understanding" about Alvernia's Catholic identity, the principles of Catholic Social Teaching, and Franciscan identity, including the core values. It emphasized the need for greater intentionality regarding mission and proposed an action plan. The document acknowledged the important role of lay women and men, from Catholic and other faith backgrounds, in ensuring a strong commitment to mission.

*Mission and Identity: A Handbook for Trustees of Catholic Colleges and Universities* (ACCU, 2003) contains these two very helpful articles: Ingram, Richard T. "The challenges of mission and identity" (p. 15–21) and Morey, Melanie and Dennis H. Holtschneider, C.M., "The meaning and patterns of Catholic sponsorship today," (p. 53-60).

### The Sponsorship Learning Community (SLC)

As the FLC undertook its work, the board of trustees engaged in a multi-year series of educational plenary sessions exploring Catholic and Franciscan identity: presentations by visiting scholars on *Ex corde Ecclesiae*; the history and diversity of American Catholic higher education; Franciscan theology, spirituality, and education; and trends in sponsorship and church-campus interactions. With a board diverse in religious backgrounds, and with even Catholic trustees unfamiliar with canon law and the rationale and workings of the university's two-tier governance system, a more systemic approach seemed advisable. The dramatic demographic challenges facing Catholic religious congregations and the Vatican II call for lay-religious collaboration made it imperative that congregational and trustee leaders have deeply shared understanding and commitment to the university. The exceptionally warm, collegial relationships among the congregational minister, board chair, and president also made the timing ideal for a creative initiative.

Proposed by the president, established jointly by the board chair and the congregational minister, the Sponsorship Learning Community (SLC) was launched in July 2010. The group brought together the five members of the congregational leadership team and five lay trustees. The SLC was chaired by a Franciscan sister-trustee who is also a respected university president. Initially the group was staffed by the president, with assistance from the interim mission officer.

See, for example, Smith, Rosemary S.C., Warren Brown, O.M.I., and Nancy Reynolds, S.P. (Eds.). *Sponsorship in the United States Context: Theory and Praxis.* Canon Law Society of America, 2006.

The SLC met bi-monthly, learning the components of sponsorship from various perspectives. Two canon lawyers provided historical perspective on the evolution of sponsorship as well as an introduction to the key canons applicable to higher education. Members discussed the principles of *Ex corde Ecclesiae* and its *U.S. Application.* They also learned about the history and current ministries of the sponsoring congregation. Trustees and congregational leaders shared expectations for themselves and each other. At the end of the first year, with new congregational leaders due to be selected, the SLC reported their upcoming agenda to the board of trustees:

- Continue to build collegial relationships among the new congregational leaders, the board, and the president;
- Begin the groundwork for development of a "sponsorship agreement" and the review of the university's bylaws.

With new congregational leaders in place in October 2011 and the Special Assistant for Mission Integration and Education assuming office in January 2012, all agreed to begin work on a "sponsorship covenant." Their goal was to finish the work of the SLC by June 2013.

The elongated schedule enabled a smooth transition—for the new mission officer, the congregational leaders, and the entire SLC. As a Franciscan scholar and a former member of both the congregational leadership team and the board of trustees, the special assistant was well suited to assume responsibility for implementing the recommendations of the FLC report. She was able to facilitate the development of mission integration plans for the various areas of the university in collaboration with a Mission Integration team of faculty and administrators, as well as with her fellow executives. As staff to the board's mission committee, she was prepared to provide continuing education to those members and engage them in active oversight of mission-related initiatives. Most importantly, she assumed responsibility for managing the complex processes needed to conceive and write a Sponsorship Covenant and to revise the "reserved powers" in the bylaws.

The Sponsorship Covenant, approved by the Board of Trustees in December 2012, could not have been envisioned when the SLC convened. It was intentionally designed to be a "relational" rather than a legal document: one blending inspiration with pledges of commitment and accountability. Review of comparable documents helped inform the shape and structure of the document around "mutual expectations." Led by the Special Assistant for Mission, a core working group—consisting of the congregational minister, chair of the board of trustees, university president, and the convener of the SLC—drafted a document. It was revised following feedback by the SLC, reviewed by the mission committee of the board, and reviewed again by the full board, before being formally approved in December 2012.

> Especially helpful was the sponsorship document titled *Covenant* from St. Catherine's University in Minnesota, which provided a framework for how to approach the creation of a new sponsorship document. Its structure and collegial perspective gave clarity to the desire to move forward with the sponsorship covenant project at Alvernia (Sisters of St. Joseph of Carondelet Governance Task Force, St. Paul Province and St. Catherine University, 2007–2009).

Work reviewing the bylaws involved the same working group, with involvement of the legal counsels for both the university and the congregation. The reserved powers were consolidated and updated. Following review by the members of the SLC, the revisions were approved by the board of trustees in June 2013.

## Six Lessons Learned

The Alvernia experience yields six lessons to guide similar processes at other institutions.

- *Recognize significant differences among the cultures of religious congregations, boards of trustees, and university communities.* Conversations about sponsorship are complex and multi-layered, involving legitimate concerns and worries as well as shared values and commitments. Differences in leadership styles and the pace of deliberations must be respected, especially since lay presidents seldom have experience working with congregational leaders, and mission officers have limited experience working with faculty.

- *Build relationships first.* Trust among the congregational minister, board chair, and president was essential for the creation of the SLC. Midway through the process, the decision to allow ample time for the new congregational leadership team to get to know trustees before beginning work was critical to the final results.

- *Form a learning community, not a committee.* The SLC and FLC were successful because of their dedication to intensive study, reflection, and dialogue *before* any planning or reports were begun. Shared inquiry shaped shared commitments.

- *Nurture genuine working partnerships.* Whether board chair and president, president and congregational leader, or small working groups, work on sponsorship requires cultivation of multiple partnerships.
- *Recognize that sponsorship is in essence about "right relationships" and shared values.* Bylaws are important. Governance must be handled effectively and efficiently. But sponsorship is ultimately about high ideals, mutual trust, respectful partnerships, and passionate commitment to mission.
- *Articulate the complementary roles of president and mission officer.* No one except the president can be the *chief* mission officer, but a mission-centered president needs a strong, credible mission officer to ensure sustained progress … and results.

*Thomas F. Flynn is President and Professor of English, Alvernia University, Reading, PA.*

*Sr. Roberta A. McKelvie, OSF is Assistant to the President for Mission Integration and Education at Alvernia University, Reading, PA.*

## chapter TWENTY-FOUR
••••••

### Marianist Educational Associates: Common Guidelines

*compiled and edited by Thomas Giardino, SM*

### Introduction

In 2005 members from all three Marianist universities responded to the call from the Association of Marianist Universities (AMU) Board to build a partnership between members of the Society of Mary, the sponsoring religious body, and a cadre of lay collaborators that would together sustain and renew the mission and identity that was Catholic and that embodied our Marianist educational tradition.[1] The first cohort of Marianist Educational Associates (MEA) entered into an initial formation program and the adventure began.

In 2009 the AMU Board and a group of MEAs reviewed the activities, initiatives, and efforts of the initial years and made plans for growing this movement of lay leadership for Catholic and Marianist mission and identity of our Marianist universities. Among the recommendations developed and accepted was a revision of the original statement of the Core Commitments and an exploration of common guidelines for the MEA experience at all the universities.

At the 2012 Strategic Directions retreat of the AMU Board, the development of common guidelines was given high priority. The present text was developed and approved by the AMU Board on October 15, 2013 after consultation with MEAs, the Sponsorship Officers (Rector/VP for Mission) and the AMU Board.

### Rationale and Purpose of the MEA Initiative

In times of rapid social change, Father Chaminade, founder of the Society of Mary, encouraged members and communities of the Marianist family to enter into what today we call "dialogues of faith and culture." He encouraged and modeled these dialogues using the light of faith to critically probe these social changes to understand the deep unmet human needs present within them. At the same time, he showed the ways we can let insights contained or manifested within social change help the community recover basic understandings of the Christian faith tradition. In this way, we can incorporate these insights into a new model for rebuilding and transforming the Church and society.

As the AMU Board probed the situation of our Marianist universities, it was clear that the Holy Spirit was calling us to something new. The consolidation and revitalization of four Provinces of the Society of Mary into one Marianist Province of the United

---

1  *In 2004, the AMU Board approved a proposal and rationale for the creation of the MEA initiative.*

States has given our three universities one common sponsoring religious community. The formation of the new Province has brought about innovation in the way the Society of Mary sponsors its universities, new modes of collaboration, and a more flexible pool of religious for the Society's ministry of higher education. Although fewer Marianist religious will be available for higher education ministry in the future, the Province has undertaken a new sponsorship structure to collaborate more effectively with the boards, administrators, staffs, and volunteers at its universities. Included in this project is an ongoing formation effort aimed at sustaining the gift of Blessed Chaminade and the Marianist educational tradition into the future.

To ensure that Marianist universities sustain a strong Catholic and Marianist mission and identity, it was important to accomplish three vital tasks. First, there must be a significant number of persons who are employed at the universities who are steeped in and appreciate the Catholic and Marianist traditions of education. Second, these persons must have the capacity and willingness to work together to incorporate these traditions into the culture of Marianist universities. Third, these persons would be committed to adapt and transform the traditions so that Marianist universities forge an engaging response to the challenges facing American higher education while contributing to the task of working toward global justice, so integral to the Marianist charism.

In order to meet the challenge of continued vitality of our Marianist universities, the Association of Marianist Universities decided to undertake the development of Marianist Educational Associates in each of the Marianist universities. To aid this development on each of our campuses, the board of the AMU developed a working definition and some characteristics of Marianist Educational Associates.

Marianist Educational Associates are members of a professional community intentionally committed to strengthening, developing, and advancing the Catholic and Marianist mission and identity of Marianist universities. Marianist Educational Associates support one another in growing in the knowledge and appreciation of the Catholic and Marianist educational traditions. They also work together to incorporate these traditions into the culture of Marianist universities and to adapt and transform these traditions so they are responsive to the challenges facing our Marianist universities. Individuals from all sectors of our Marianist universities are invited to be Marianist Educational Associates.[2]

## Core Commitments of the Marianist Educational Associates Common to All Three Universities

1. *All MEAs strive to be a professional presence on the campus that promotes the Catholic and Marianist mission and identity of our Marianist-sponsored University.*

> MEAs are lay persons who are, first of all, employees of the campus community that are hired to perform in a professional role in the work of Marianist higher education. MEAs make an intentional choice to use that professional role to partner with the Marianist vowed religious on campus to strengthen the Catholic and Marianist mission and identity. All MEAs are committed to using their sphere of influence to strengthen the Catholic and Marianist mission and identity in ways that are effective and appropriate, i.e., in ways that respect subsidiarity and

---

2  *Much of this text and the following regarding the Core Commitments are based on the work of Raymond Fitz, SM, first Executive Director of the AMU, based on conversations with MEAs and the AMU Board.*

the university organization. MEAs are committed to a journey of personal and professional growth in understanding and embracing the gift of the Marianist charism.

2. *All MEAs are committed to ongoing learning about the Catholic and Marianist traditions as they apply to higher education.*

For MEAs to be effective and know how to operate in an appropriate Marianist style, it is important for them to know and appreciate the Catholic and Marianist traditions as they apply to higher education. MEAs participate in initial and ongoing formation programs that introduce them to and deepen their appreciation of important concepts and themes of Catholic and Marianist higher education. MEAs develop a sense of the Catholic and Marianist traditions as living traditions and as historical realities that change and develop as the people of Marianist-sponsored universities confront new challenges. MEAs, in partnership with the Marianist religious, work to develop and enrich these traditions.

3. *The MEAs are committed to forming a community of challenge and support with other MEAs that strives to embody and give witness to the Catholic and Marianist traditions of education.*

In the Marianist tradition, personal commitments are strengthened and enriched in a challenging and supportive community. MEAs form a community on their campus for the sake of sustaining one another in their commitment to strengthen the Catholic and Marianist mission and identity of the university. These communities develop appropriate means of organizing themselves. The MEA communities also develop appropriate means to hold each other accountable for their commitments and to assist one another in carrying out important tasks that the community decides to undertake.

4. *All MEAs are committed to being part of a university community of positive influence on campus that is engaged in reading the signs of the times and learning to utilize the Catholic and Marianist traditions in forging responses to these signs.*

MEAs as individuals and as a community endeavor to positively influence the university culture, especially as that culture supports the Catholic and Marianist mission and identity and engages it in initiatives responsive to the signs of the times. Collectively, MEAs are cultural catalysts on campus by being attentive to issues, by deliberating on options for change, by organizing people and marshaling resources to bring about the intended change, and by learning from the change through reflection. Being a cultural catalyst requires respect for the university as an institution of higher education and learning how to work within the organization in an appropriate manner. For example, it is important to respect subsidiarity and thus to address the problem or issue at a level where the decision maker has responsibility for this problem or issue. Accordingly, it is important for MEAs to continually develop the skills of being a cultural catalyst.

5. *All MEAs make a public affirmation to live their commitment as MEAs.*

MEAs make an annual public affirmation within the university community to live their commitments. This public affirmation gives witness to their fellow MEAs and to others on the campus that they want to continue this journey of understanding and growth in the Catholic and Marianist traditions of higher education and that they want to be held accountable for this commitment.

Core Commitments but different journeys: The five Core Commitments outlined above define part of what is common to all MEAs in Marianist-sponsored universities, recognizing that there will be some processes and practices proper to each university. The MEA commitment does not require a person to be a Catholic or a Christian; but it says that the person making the MEA commitment strongly affirms many of the basic beliefs, practices, and norms of the Catholic and Marianist traditions of higher education and wants to work at incorporating them into the culture of the Marianist-sponsored universities. Some MEAs may decide to explore further the Marianist charism, with its spirituality and apostolic methods, and become a member of a Marianist Lay Community or an affiliate of the Society of Mary or Daughters of Mary Immaculate.

## The Association of Marianist Universities and the Marianist Educational Associates

The Association of Marianist Universities — established in 2003 — is the collaborative organization that aims to support, promote, and advance Marianist higher education. The AMU does this by facilitating an environment to sustain cooperation and the exchange of experience and information among the members.

The AMU is the primary sponsor of the MEA initiative, though it is ordinarily lived out on the individual campus. As sponsor, the AMU fosters, supports, and oversees the development of the MEAs as a network of persons committed to enhancing the mission of Marianist universities. To this end, the AMU takes responsibility for programs of initial and ongoing formation of MEAs that complement those of the local university. The president and the sponsorship officer of each university select the candidates and notify the members of the university. As a symbol of the partnership with the AMU, the AMU Executive Director sends a letter of acceptance to each person selected to enter the initial formation program. Upon making their initial public commitment, MEAs receive a pin common to all Marianist Educational Associates. Also, a common MEA information piece will be developed and will be available on the AMU website.

## Common Guidelines for Recruitment and Selection of MEAs

1. For consideration to be an MEA, one must be a full-time employee of a Marianist university at the time of one's initial commitment. MEAs who move to formal "Emeritus" status may continue to be considered as MEAs upon mutual agreement with the sponsorship officer.

2. To be considered for MEA selection, one must have been employed for at least three years in one of the Marianist universities or related Marianist institution. In the latter case, the AMU Executive Director approves the exception.

3. Information and invitation to apply to be an MEA is made available to all in the university; how this happens may be different at each university.

4. The selection process begins with the sponsorship officer and includes the dean, vice president or supervisor of the person and ends with the president and sponsorship officer approving.

5. Ordinarily, the yearly number eligible for initial formation from each university

is as follows: Chaminade University of Honolulu, 4-5; St. Mary's, 7-9; University of Dayton, 9-11. Actual numbers will depend on circumstances.

6. If it remains the candidate's intent, one becomes an MEA after participation in and the successful completion of the initial formation program sponsored by the AMU. This includes making the MEA statement of commitment during the closing ceremony.

7. Some characteristics of a person to be considered as an MEA are:

a. Already involved in strengthening the Catholic and Marianist mission of the university.

b. Is well-respected by their colleagues and supervisors for their professional performance.

c. Demonstrates a collaborative spirit.

d. Demonstrates an ability to impact others in their sphere of influence.

e. Is likely to continue regular and active participation in MEA activities past the first year and has the flexibility and commitment to participate in ongoing formation.

f. Respects the Catholic and Marianist traditions.

## Common Rituals and Practices Across the Campuses

1. A public commitment ceremony for a new MEA happens within the first year after the initial formation program on the "home" campus.
2. The timing of the ceremony is a matter for individual campus decision.
3. The common elements of the ceremony are the following:

    a. The ceremony is to be in the context of a prayer service or liturgy open to the university community.

    b. For the initial public commitment by an MEA, he or she would state his/her commitment individually; in subsequent years, this may be stated as a cohort or other grouping, since the numbers are growing larger.

    c. The individual and group statement of commitment, received by the sponsorship officer, is based on the five Core Commitments common to all three Marianist universities and is as follows:

*As a Marianist Educational Associate, I pledge [renew my pledge] to strengthen, sustain and develop the Catholic and Marianist mission and identity of _____. I will continue to read, reflect, and collaborate with others to insure the continuation of the programs, processes, and behaviors that make us a Catholic and Marianist University.*

*I promise to support others in growing in the knowledge and appreciation of our Catholic and Marianist traditions in order to embody and witness to these traditions and their benefit to our world.*

*Furthermore, I promise to give myself to the larger community as fully as possible by remaining spiritually present, alive, and open to the call of the Marianist charism as I am personally able.*

4. A symbol in the form of a pin common to all the universities is given to each MEA at the time of their initial public commitment.

## Organizational and Ongoing Formation Matters

Along with regular participation in their campus MEA activities, MEAs are expected to continue their formation in local and/or national ongoing activities of growth and development.

At least once every three years, each MEA meets with the sponsorship officer to discuss their participation and possibilities in MEA life on campus. The sponsorship officer initiates the conversation.

Each campus develops some structure of leadership and organization (e.g., a coordinator or coordinating team) which promotes participation, responsibility, subsidiarity, and accountability. This structure is accountable to the sponsorship officer.

If an MEA decides not to renew their annual commitment, they cease to be a part of the MEA community. If an MEA is not able to renew their commitment with the group due to circumstances, then he or she works out a specific arrangement to renew it (e.g., signing the commitment pledge) with the sponsorship officer.

In extenuating circumstances, an MEA may ask for a leave of absence from the MEA community. After one year, the MEA, in dialogue with the sponsorship officer, makes a decision to continue as an MEA or to leave the program.

If an MEA moves to employment in another Marianist university, he or she may become a part of that MEA group by mutual consent with the sponsorship officers.

The sponsorship officer, upon due consideration and with the approval of the president, may in extraordinary circumstances dismiss a member of the MEA community for conduct inimical or contrary to the MEA Core Commitments, Catholic and Marianist traditions, or the mission and identity of the university.

The MEA programs at the local and national levels reflect ecumenical and interfaith/interreligious sensibilities as integral to the Catholic and Marianist tradition.

## Conclusion

"If we intend to do business by halves, it will not be worth the while to take so much trouble. ... Above all I am determined to form really good establishments, before being solicitous about their numbers." (Blessed William Joseph Chaminade, *Letters*, vol.1, no. 202 to Mertian, June 18, 1822)

This foundational intent of Fr. Chaminade finds continuity in the vision of the Association of Marianist Universities to bring together "the diverse gifts of each of the campuses into a dynamic network that enables the Marianist universities to be leaders in American higher education." Marianist Educational Associates are one of these diverse gifts and the fruit of these really good establishments. They take the trouble to learn and embrace the Catholic and Marianist traditions of higher education personally and professionally for the sake of the common good of the Church and world.

These MEA Common Guidelines are an attempt to assist MEAs in their desires to live fully – not by "halves" – their Core Commitments. The Commitments are challenging, but MEAs are not alone in the journey. God's Spirit and Mary, patroness of each Marianist university, are with each MEA and MEA community. Also, the witness of gifted and committed colleagues in service of others inspires and supports the MEA movement along the way. To this purpose, the Common Guidelines is a living document and will evolve as the MEA journey develops and flourishes.

*Compiled and edited by Thomas F. Giardino, SM, who is Executive Director of the Association of Marianist Universities.*

# section FIVE
● ● ● ● ● ●

**Hiring for Mission Across the University**

# chapter TWENTY-FIVE
● ● ● ● ● ●

## Asking the Right Questions When Hiring for Mission

*Marguerite O'Beirne, OSF*

Since the publication of *Ex corde Ecclesiae*, an apostolic constitution on Catholic universities by Pope John Paul II, there has been increased conversation, study, and research on how to preserve and strengthen the unique Catholic identity and purpose of Catholic higher education in the United States. Of foremost importance is the hiring practice of an institution:

"If Catholic universities are to succeed in their missions, the question of who gets chosen to be a laborer in their work … is of great importance" (Araujo, 1999, p. 835). Given the significance of this issue for the work of the mission officer in each institution of Catholic higher education, it is of utmost importance that a priority be given to the mission officer to put in place structures and practices for hiring staff, faculty, and administrators in light of the religious purpose of the institution. Working closely with the human resources administrator on these practices is essential for successful hiring protocol.

*Ex corde Ecclesiae* affirms this focus when it states that "the responsibility for maintaining and strengthening the Catholic identity of the university … is shared in varying degrees by all members of the university community, and therefore calls for the recruitment of adequate university personnel, especially teachers and administrators, who are both willing and able to promote that identity" (II, 4.1). The document reaffirms this when it states that "all teachers and all administrators, at the time of their appointment, are to be informed about the Catholic identity of the institution and its implications and about their responsibility to promote, or at least to respect, that identity" (II, 4.2). Neumann University believes that the candidate and the university are served well if Catholic identity and university mission questions are best handled well before "the time of the appointment."

The responsibility of the mission officer is clear: the mission officer assists the institution in hiring a sufficient number of personnel who have the ability to support and promote the religious purpose of the university. This responsibility, of maintaining the spirit and unique religious culture, has become even more urgent with the gradual diminishment of the members of founding religious congregations who were once the core group on campus.

## Neumann University's Hiring Process

Attentive to the signs of the time, the mandates from Church documents, and the desire to strengthen the Catholic Franciscan mission, Neumann University developed an institution-wide process with specific tools to assist search committees in the hiring process. This *Resource Guide for Mission-Centered Hiring*, developed by the Office of Mission and Ministry in collaboration with the Human Resources Office, assists all interviewers and members of search committees with questions that explore the candidate's familiarity with the university's mission, vision, and core values. This tool, developed in consultation with input from members of the university community, has now been included in the university's policies for hiring.

All advertisements of the position descriptions include the statement: "Candidates must possess an appreciation for and congruence with the Catholic Franciscan mission of the University" (http://www.neumann.edu/about/humanresources/employment.asp). The Human Resources Office provides the Mission-Centered Hiring packet to each search committee. During the pre-interview process, candidates are invited to review the university's Identity, Mission, and Values statements with a list of the Core Values from the university's webpage. This packet enables the candidate at the outset to determine his or her own fit for the institution and to prepare for mission-related questions during the interview process.

Some search committees have found it helpful to have a specific member of the committee ask mission-related questions. Faculty candidates are asked to submit a written statement describing their understanding of the mission of a liberal arts, faith-based institution, and how they will support the mission in their discipline.

The Mission-Centered Hiring packet includes several questions designed to clarify the intent of the hiring-for-mission process for the search committee and the candidate.

1. *Must all candidates be Catholic or Christian?* No. It is not necessary to be Catholic or Christian, but it is important that candidates express their ability to support the Catholic Franciscan educational mission in Neumann University's search for truth as expressed in the mission statement.

2. *Won't mission-centered hiring practices stifle individuality and contribute to a homogeneous rather than a heterogeneous faculty and staff?* No. We believe that in the context of pursuing truth, justice, and excellence, there is room for great diversity. Additionally, such diversity ensures ongoing dialogue as we pursue truth and knowledge. This dialogue helps foster awareness of both the possibilities and limitations of our own heritage.

3. *How would asking mission-related questions be helpful?* By encouraging candidates to reflect on the mission statement's values and ideals, they can assess their potential for contributing to and benefiting from the university's mission.

4. *Won't mission-centered hiring simply turn into a "litmus test" to assess the orthodoxy of candidates according to whatever interpretation is prevalent?* Mission-centered hiring is not a religious litmus test for any particular manifestation of Catholic belief. Rather, the process encourages a mutually beneficial relationship, supporting the candidate's pursuit for self-fulfillment and the university's quest to live out its mission.

The packet suggests helpful interview questions and the rationale for asking these questions. The wording and tone in which these questions are asked can make a significant difference in how the candidate interprets the institution's seriousness regarding its mission. While the following questions do not have right or wrong answers, they are intended to assist the search committee and the mission officer to determine the candidate's "fit" for the religious mission and values of the institution. While each mission officer or search committee may wish to craft specific questions that reflect the institution's unique mission and vision, here is a sampling of some used in the interview:

1. *What aspects of the mission statement appeal to you?*

2. *How do you think the university mission and Catholic identity of (name of university) will support the work you do as a professor/ staff / administrator?*

3. *Do any aspects of the mission statement cause you concern?*

4. (For faculty candidates) *(Name of university) affirms the connection between faith and reason in the search for truth. What are your thoughts about the relationship between faith and reason in the academy?*

Responses to these questions usually provide a good indication of a candidate's comfort level with the Catholic mission of the university.

Mission officers work to engage the entire university community. "The university community of many Catholic institutions includes members of other Churches, ecclesial communities and religions, and also those who profess no religious belief" (*Ex corde Ecclesiae*, II, 26). This challenges mission officers to ensure that the Catholic core of faculty, staff, and administrators are well prepared in their knowledge of the Catholic tradition, so that the Catholic identity and founding charism of the sponsoring congregations are preserved and strengthened into the future.

Finding the right candidate to fill the position who is both qualified and committed to mission is important. Equally important is the ongoing formation and evaluation of faculty, staff, and administration during their beginning years at the university. These formation programs are particularly important because eventually some of the newly hired faculty will be applying for tenure. During the faculty tenure process we revisit these questions by reviewing the faculty member's engagement in mission formation programs offered throughout the years and how the mission and values of the institution have been integrated in one's area of discipline.

Subsequent to hiring, therefore, it is important to provide ongoing formation. This formation often takes two forms: programmatic and individualized. Programmatic designs could include evenings or afternoons of reflection, seminars, immersion experiences, retreats, or retracing the footsteps of the founder

The Ignatian Mentoring Program at Xavier University is a yearlong program wherein senior faculty assist new faculty to incorporate a mission-driven teaching component into their courses. http://www.xavier.edu/mission-identity/programs/ignatian-mentoring-program.cfm.

• • • • • • • • • • • • • • • • • • • • • • • • • • • • • •

programs. Individualized mentoring on Catholic identity, charism, or university mission can take the shape of one-on-one sharings with the mission officer, a member of the mission committee, a university mission mentor, or a member of the sponsoring religious community. Individual conversations on mission and identity that emerge from the new employee questions are often the most productive.

The question, "How does one effectively hire for mission?" is a critical one for all mission officers in Catholic colleges and universities. The intent of hiring-for-mission policies is to provide assistance and guidance in answering that question as we take on the responsibility of strengthening and sustaining the distinctive identity of Catholic colleges and universities into the future.

*Sr. Marguerite O'Beirne, OSF is Vice President Mission and Ministry at Neumann University, Aston, PA.*

---

*Reference*

Araujo, R. (1999). "*Ex corde Ecclesiae* and Mission-Centered Hiring in Roman Catholic Colleges and Universities: To Boldly Go Where We Have Gone Before." *The Journal of College and University Law*, 25(4), 835-864.

## chapter TWENTY-SIX

## Engaging Departmental Faculty Early in Mission-Centered Hiring

*Kevin Hughes*

One of the most important and yet most difficult issues for a mission officer to handle is the question of hiring faculty. Often any input from a mission officer is received by department faculty as, at best, irrelevant to the search that they are conducting, or, at worst, the heavy-handed intrusion of administrative authority and a violation of academic freedom. These conversations can quickly and easily become rhetorically overheated and counterproductive. The sensitivity is heightened in the hiring process because, quite simply, hiring is always a crucial moment of re-founding and re-imagining. The stakes are very high. From the mission officer's perspective, the hiring question is one of the most important dimensions to the flourishing life of the Catholic mission at his or her institution. Yet the mission officer may feel entirely helpless in this crucial activity. A few steps can be taken early in the process to avoid some of these live-wire scenarios. If mission officers can engage departmental faculty in a conversation about the relationship of the department to the institution's mission, and facilitate the composition of a heuristic document that conveys that relationship, the foundation is laid for a more productive conversation about particular searches and particular hires.

The initial conversation between a mission officer and a department can be part of a broader initiative asking departments to develop a statement of the relationship of their discipline(s) and departmental work to the Catholic mission of the institution as a whole. The mission officer's role in the conversation is primarily that of resource support, to help faculty describe the methods and ends of their particular field or discipline in a way that can connect with the terms and principles of the Catholic mission. Departmental faculty are presumed to be experts in what their field seeks to know or produce, but we cannot assume that they have ever had an opportunity to link those ends, in concrete and specific ways, to the institution's mission. Faculty may not agree about the methods and ends of their discipline; still it would be valuable for them to connect their discipline to the mission in ways they deem possible. Placing this conversation in the context of a broader notion of mission may help to create common ground. For example, different ends formulated by mathematicians and statisticians may be better understood together in the context of a broader desire to know, as articulated in a Catholic vision of education.

The mission officer can assist departments with the work of developing the statement by asking questions that proceed from the specific to the general. The conversation might begin with a focused discussion of the particular department's own sense of its pedagogical

The mission and ministry office at DePaul University funds quarterly Catholic Intellectual Tradition conversations. Individuals from different departments are responsible for identifying the topic, selecting an article to serve as a conversation starting point, and recruiting colleagues who explore dimensions of the Catholic Intellectual Tradition in small groups from a variety of disciplines and perspectives. http://www.accunet. org/i4a/member_directory/feResultsDetail. cfm?directory_id=27&detail_lookup_id=948.

• • • • • • • • • • • • • • • • • • • • • • • • • • • • • • •

goals and objectives: What do we hope to help our students do, see, understand, or become? What skills and knowledge are entailed in the training that we give to them? These conclusions should then be placed in a slightly larger frame: How do these specific goals contribute to the overall goals of the school? An accounting department might delineate the various skills needed in accounting, but then speak to how those skills fit within the larger goals of a school of business. This could then lead to reflection on the role of a school of business in a Catholic vision of human flourishing in economy and society. Once this layer of reflection is added, it would be fruitful to return to the specific goals articulated by the department: How does accounting, then, contribute to a Catholic vision of human flourishing in economy and society? It is at this point that the mission officer's input is most valuable, in introducing faculty to the Catholic Intellectual Tradition with a specific eye to its contributions to or intersection with disciplinary and departmental goals, and in helping faculty think through these connections to Catholic mission in a creative and constructive way. A mission statement that shows good mission-oriented reasons for doing the things already detailed by the faculty as specific disciplinary goals will help to bridge the perceived gap between abstract or idealistic "mission-talk" and the real business of an academic discipline.

The role of the mission officer, with a department that has already formulated a mission statement of its own, could be to revisit that statement and offer input on it in specific relation to the institutional mission. Doing so, under the banner of preparing a department for a faculty search, will have the effect of "focusing the mind" in a way different from the sometimes detached activity of composing a departmental mission statement. Whether revisiting an existing document or starting from

Global Business Institute for Societal Responsibility, based at St. Edward's University, focuses on faculty and students working together to create socially responsible, implementable solutions for people anywhere in the world. http://www.accunet. org/i4a/member_directory/feResultsDetail. cfm?directory_id=27&detail_lookup_id=1006.

• • • • • • • • • • • • • • • • • • • • • • • • • • • • • • •

scratch, the mission officer would need to present the mission in its most generous terms. The Catholic view of the reciprocal and interdependent relationship between faith and reason, wherein reason's natural powers to know are understood not to be in conflict with the tenets and practice of faith, and wherein seeking truth according to the canons of rational inquiry are essential to a deep understanding of the human good, should be stated first. This broadest level of understanding creates the space for rational inquiry of all sorts; every discipline represents some sort of inquiry and so fits within the capacious vision of a Catholic college or university.

Beyond this, Catholic commitments to social justice and to the common good may be helpful in articulating the mission-role to more applied fields of knowledge in schools of business, education, engineering, law, medicine, or nursing. At an even deeper level of specificity, the particular mission of an institution (Augustinian, Benedictine, Franciscan, Jesuit, Salesian, etc.) may be of use in generating a deeper relationship still. Again, the mission officer's role in this conversation is to offer these points of connection after she or he has heard from the faculty their own understanding of their discipline's methods and ends. Listening is essential; one suspicion that faculty may have of mission officers is that they try to filter every discipline through the sieve of a ready-made understanding of the mission. To the extent that this conversation can truly be reciprocal and exploratory, it will be more successful and will provide an opportunity for both faculty and mission officers to learn.

The Augustinian Pilgrimage, preceded by six weeks of readings and held over the October break, is a prayerful journey through Italy. It deepens a pilgrim's understanding of Villanova University's Catholic identity and Augustinian heritage of Veritas, Unitas, and Caritas. http://www.accunet.org/i4a/member_directory/feResultsDetail.cfm?directory_id=27&detail_lookup_id=978.

Of course, all of the above should be taken with the caveat that some departments and disciplines will have greater levels of specificity than others in their articulation of mission. A department of philosophy will clearly have more to say than a department of accounting, because the discipline of philosophy *as philosophy* concerns the love of wisdom and consideration of reason's power to know, whereas accounting *as accounting* may not have anything explicitly to say about these fundamental issues. But even in this case, a department of accounting can be understood *as a contributor to a school of business*, the ends of which can be clearly and intimately related to notions of social and economic flourishing and proper business ethics as articulated in Catholic social thought and moral theology. The level of specificity in a departmental statement of mission will vary according to discipline.

With this conversation completed and a document or statement formulated, the next step of the process becomes clearer. When departments seek to hire, they can be asked to communicate the need for this search *in terms of the department's own statement of its relation to the institution's mission*. Since the prior conversation has taken place, the need to "reinvent" a rationale on the occasion of each search is diminished, and certain terms and touchstones have already been identified. The very design and language of the job description and request for permission to hire can and ought already to reflect and engage with the department's role in the institution's mission. This should be a process shared by the whole department, but one might consider appointing the search committee at this early stage in the process. The committee's first task would be to draft the job description and request to hire, bringing these drafts to the rest of the department for review and revision. Indeed, the hard work of relating the particular job to the departmental mission is the best sort of preparation for the search committee's review of candidates. At this stage the mission officer's role is ideally that of consultant and resource person, helping the committee to bridge any perceived gap between the particular needs of the job and their own departmental statement. The last stage of this process is the search itself. Many Catholic institutions have begun to include a requirement for applicants to respond to the institution's mission in a document to be included in their dossier. Depending on the applicant and discipline, such a response can seem abstract from the candidate's point of view. Responses in these cases often boil down to "I have a commitment to teaching and not just research" or "Service is important." Instead the department's own statement of its relationship to the university mission should be included in the materials offered to the applicant. The applicant is asked to respond to this statement, discussing both how her or his current research and teaching may conform with the department's vision, and how she or he may anticipate developing that research and teaching in ways that both learn from and contribute to the vision. Due to the statement's direct relationship to their own discipline, this should be an easier step for most applicants. At the same time, it provides a more useful tool for assessment of applicants, both at the departmental level and for deans and other administrators. It is unfair to ask applicants to do the work of articulating the significance of their discipline, research, and teaching, to the institutional mission as a whole. These intermediate documents provide an easier point of access to the applicant and a more precise assessment tool for the review and interview process.

Consulting early in the hiring process has many significant advantages.

- It allows time and place for departments to become conscious of and formulate their sense of their discipline within the context of the institutional mission as a whole.

- It places the mission officer from the start in the role of consultant and resource person, and hopefully it provides ground for a fruitful conversation with give and take.

- It gives departments an important tool to be used in the rationale for their own petitions to hire, and it provides deans and/or provosts with the same tool by which to evaluate the request.

- It adds a focused and specific element to the application and review process, which can be a useful diagnostic tool for both departments and administrators in evaluating candidates.

- Generally, and perhaps more importantly, it places the hiring process in the immediate and explicit light of a discussion of mission; a discussion more detailed and specific than the larger institutional mission statement will permit. Mission-centered hiring criteria cannot then be seen as extrinsic to the discipline-specific criteria described by a departmental faculty. Since the mission-centered criteria have already been internalized and addressed by the departmental faculty, the soil for a more fruitful harvest of mission-friendly hiring has been prepared.

A process like this yields a more efficient and useful tool for the hiring of faculty. It leads to an understanding of the relationship between departments, disciplines, and mission that is more in keeping with Catholic principles in general, that faith has no enemy in the truth, and that we seek to embrace truth wherever and however it may be found.

*Kevin Hughes is Chair, Department of Humanities and Classical Studies Program, Director, Patristic, Medieval, and Renaissance Studies Conference (PMR), Associate Professor, Theology and Religious Studies at Villanova University, Villanova, PA.*

## chapter TWENTY-SEVEN

**The Role of the Mission Officer during the Faculty Interview Process**

*Lisa Mary McCartney, RSM*

An extraordinary year of faculty hiring at Mercyhurst, a comprehensive Catholic university of just over 4,000 students and 190 faculty members, inspired this chapter. In the hiring process, it is the mission officer's primary responsibility to evaluate the mission fit of potential faculty members, indeed to look for optimal community fits. Toward this goal, Mercyhurst has found personal interviews to be the most effective means of evaluating candidates.

### 2008-2011: From Limited to Significant Participation in the Hiring Process

The Office of Mission Integration was created at the university in 2008. A member of the sponsoring religious community, who was also a tenured faculty member, was appointed to the position of Vice President for Mission Integration. She reports to the president of the university and assists him in promoting and animating the university's mission as expressed in its mission statement. In 2008, the president directed that new vice president to be included in the faculty hiring process. As a whole, faculty chairs responded positively, admitting inadequacies in discussing mission with candidates. However, her inclusion in their hiring process proved to be uneven at best until 2011 when the Office of Academic Affairs instituted a hiring protocol. Having the Office of Academic Affairs manage the entire hiring process changed the status of the mission officer, enabling her to make a significant impact on campus. Formalizing processes regarding mission issues, such as hiring, makes a profound difference in effectiveness.

Since Mercyhurst was looking to fill some twenty-five vacancies during the course of the academic year 2011-2012, OAA wisely standardized the procedure for hiring faculty. It set guidelines for approval to hire, ads and their placement, full department participation, responsibilities of the search committee, and campus interviews. It specifically incorporated a minimum of a half-hour interview with the Vice President for Mission Integration into the list of administrator interviews and allocated enough singular time to enable significant conversation to occur.

### The Mission Interview Environment and Elements

Opening an interview with candid remarks about the relatively new phenomenon of a mission office in Catholic higher education, explaining both the rationale for a mission interview and significance of mission for the university, generally puts the candidate at ease. The mission interview is most effective if done in a conversational, welcoming environment. Obviously, the substance of the interview aims to help candidates see the university through the lens of its Catholic and sponsoring legacy. It is possible, and preferable, to introduce and/or interweave the topics of Catholic identity and mission into the flow of conversation. The mission officer ought to be prepared to introduce and discuss, or at least reference, such topics as:

- The sponsoring order's founder and charism focusing on its educational tradition;
- The founding of the university, its original vision and key historical moments and transitions;
- The significant concepts of the Catholic Intellectual Tradition and Catholic Social Teaching;
- Any current news or "hot button" issues about Catholic higher education and the Church.

These topics are best introduced as remarks or brief amplifications of the university's mission and core values statements, which any candidate truly interested in the position should have already considered. It is helpful to have a printed mission card at hand and use it for points of reference, and to be familiar enough with the topics to move easily around them, freely omitting some depending on the candidate's show of interest or concern and need for understanding or clarification.

A helpful strategy is to begin with a mission topic related to the candidate's field, research, or personal interests, gleaned from the vita, as well as to pick up on allusions to the website or campus visit. Many candidates enter the conversation quickly, though younger, inexperienced ones tend to be hesitant. If conversation lags, directive questions are effective: What in the mission statement (or in the core values) excites you? What in it challenges you? What in the mission would be difficult for you?

Frequently candidates, once they relax, share personal experiences and talk about their religious background and even their faith. These can be some of the most enlightening, memorable job interviews either party ever experiences. They can be the highlight of a candidate's entire visit. On occasion, candidates optimistically observe, "I am Catholic," "I was raised Catholic," "My wife is Catholic," or "I can talk about God here."

Others will admit, "I am not very religious" or "I am a spiritual person." Once a candidate remarked, "I am an agonistic so this doesn't bother me." While such an offhanded remark can make a mission officer wince, such acknowledgements can lead to a moment of mission in action where discussion of the compatibility between faith and reason or the importance of a core value can

> "It is in the context of the impartial search for truth that the relationship between faith and reason is brought to light" (*Ex corde Ecclesiae*, 5).

occur. In these moments, it is important to explore and detect the candidate's deeper intent and attitudes toward religion and faith, and see if he can appreciate and respect the mission and values of the university, even if he would not know how to advance it.

Some candidates will have little sense of faith-based higher education and will be finding their way in the academic community. They may well be open to growth in strong, mission-directed departments. If, however, a candidate is not forthcoming in talking about mission or values and keeps turning to professional and teaching matters, the mission officer ought to be wary. In an uncomfortable interview, it seems best to move to closure by asking: "Do you have any questions about the mission?" And, "I need to ask the bottom line question, could you support the mission and core values of Mercyhurst?" A mission officer will, of course, report any reservations from or about the candidate to the search committee. She shares her mission-focused impressions, trusting that her contributions are part of a respectful process, composed of multiple interviews from both faculty and administration, all aimed at determining how a candidate would fit into the educational mission of the university.

"...[A]ll teachers and all administrators, at the time of their appointment, are to be informed about the Catholic identity of the institution and its implications and about their responsibility to promote, or at least to respect, that identity" (*Ex corde Ecclesiae*, II, 4.2).

Generally, candidates who have questions about academic freedom, autonomy, or tolerance at "Catholic places" are self-possessed enough to raise them during the conversation. Often, they come from a limited understanding of the Catholic university, its centuries-long history, and the ongoing efforts of the Church and the university to understand each other's roles, as higher education has developed in America. It is the mission officer's goal to participate in the dialogue, not settle it or offer a single view. Rather, her work is to promote a mission culture, and that is a work always in progress, requiring her to illuminate the mission and core values, offer explanations of pertinent university policies, reassure candidates of both the sacred trust and autonomy of the classroom, and encourage the faculty to be friends in the work.

### Outcomes for Mission Office and Search for Faculty

With more than seventy-five interviews being conducted within a few months of 2011-2012, e-mails to the search committees expedited feedback. The "mission fit" e-mail summarized and limited the VP's observations to the candidate's responses on the overarching dimensions of mission: the Catholic identity and sponsoring community's legacy. Once the second and third candidates are met, it is natural to compare, rank, and evaluate the suitability of the pool for the university. By nature, the mission interview is a qualitative experience touching on human subjectivity and adds a holistic dimension to the search committee's evaluation.

Out of respect for the academic department and search committee, it is best to offer an opinion, not a judgment: "From a purely mission perspective this candidate is very promising" or "This candidate would have a steep mission learning curve."

The Carlow Roundtable brings together faculty and staff from Mercy colleges and universities to explore their common Mercy heritage in Ireland. Participant papers are published in the proceedings of the Roundtable and cross-campus relationships of support and collaboration are a common outcome. http://www.accunet.org/i4a/member_directory/feResultsDetail.cfm?directory_id=27&detail_lookup_id=986.

If the department decides to hire a candidate with much to learn, the mission officer should be proactive in mentoring the new member through mission-learning opportunities and conversations that go beyond those offered to new faculty. It has proven to be very worthwhile to share mission perspectives directly with the chair and the search committee, for they carry the burden and responsibility of the hiring process.

Mission interviews have multiple, even unanticipated, benefits: The new mission office gains visibility and respect from academic departments. The search committee receives an enhanced profile of the candidate, filling in missing pieces, clarifying an intuition or vague concern, or verifying an evaluation. The incoming faculty member accepts the position, realizing the importance of the mission and expecting to participate in it. Every mission officer ought to be graced with an expression of gratitude from a new hire who accepts the important role he or she will play in the university's mission.

*Sr. Lisa Mary McCartney, RSM is Vice President for Mission Integration at Mercyhurst University, Erie, PA.*

## chapter TWENTY-EIGHT
● ● ● ● ● ●

**Successful Hiring for Mission and Identity: One University's Method**

*Timothy Seaworth*

Successful hiring is all about finding the right fit. The University of Mary streamlines the process of successfully identifying persons who share the university's goals by clearly delineating the university's mission and values early in the hiring process. Ensuring faculty and staff are committed to the values of the institution is paramount to retaining good employees dedicated to transmitting mission and identity with integrity.

Since 2011, all applicants invited to interview for a position receive the university's mission and identity statements, a list of the charism/Benedictine values, and several questions which require written responses. Those who apply for senior administrative or teaching faculty positions are also asked to read and be conversant in two additional documents: *Ex corde Ecclesiae* and *Education within the Benedictine Wisdom Tradition*. This hiring method enables prospective candidates to consider the university's mission and values as well as how they can contribute to the university's mission prior to being interviewed.

This hiring method was designed in a collaborative process involving the president, the former president, the Prioress of Annunciation Monastery, members of the President's Council, the university attorney, and the human resources director. The idea came from discussions about how to use the university's newly approved statements of mission and identity and a newly formulated articulation of the university's Benedictine values in the hiring process. The goal of this method is to encourage attentive concern for the university's mission and values at all levels of the hiring process by all persons involved in the process, including the candidate. It was designed to help candidates learn not only about the extent of the mission but also the level of commitment to mission that is sought in those hired. Since 2011, the University of Mary has hired thirty employees, and this hiring method has reaped significant benefits for the university. Some outcomes include the following:

- There has been an increase in the number of mission-motivated candidates from greater distances, resulting in an increase in the overall quality of applicants;
- Candidates are more transparent during the interview process, and it is easier to ascertain what moves them, how they think about their lives, and whether they have a sense of vocation;
- There has been a savings in both time and resources regarding interview expenses because only candidates well matched to the university's mission are extended interviews;

- All finalists that meet with the university president are well vetted and prepared for any significant mission and identity issues that might be discussed.

The new process has helped us strength and streamline our hiring-for-mission initiative in significant ways.

The Hiring for Mission document details the hiring procedure and demonstrates how reflection on mission and values are integrated into the hiring process. Those interested in employment at the University of Mary are directed to the website www.umary.edu/jobs, where the candidate will find the following document:

### Hiring for Mission at the University of Mary

Those who apply for employment at the University of Mary honor us. They are enquiring about the kind of place this is. They are choosing to put themselves forward as potential members of our community. They are beginning to imagine what their future could hold if they were working here as partners for the advancement of our mission in Catholic higher education.

For these reasons the university takes seriously the responsibility to articulate our mission and values in a clear manner for applicants who have been invited to interview for a position. We also invite these applicants to respond thoughtfully to our mission and values, demonstrating how they understand them and how they might support them. This process is meant to assist the applicants in discerning whether employment at the University of Mary would be a good fit for them, whether they could be happy here.

It follows that the hiring process at the University of Mary at all levels should include meaningful conversations about mission and values, both out of courtesy and concern for the applicants and in service to the university.

### Procedure[1]

When an applicant is granted an interview, she or he is provided with:
1. a copy of this document,
2. the University of Mary statement of mission and identity,
3. the University of Mary formulation of Benedictine values.

The applicant is invited to prepare for the interview with a thoughtful, written response. Questions to consider:

- At the University of Mary, every member of the community has a role in advancing our mission. You have carefully reviewed the university's statement of mission and identity. How would you support the Christian, the Catholic, and the Benedictine mission of the University of Mary?
- Based upon the documents which have been provided to you, do you have any reservations about serving at a Catholic institution with the mission and values of the University of Mary?

---

[1] All hiring procedures at the University of Mary are to take place in accord with the university's non-discrimination statement: *The University of Mary does not discriminate on the basis of race, color, religion, sex, age, national origin, disability, marital status or public assistance, in accordance with applicable laws. The university will not tolerate any discrimination, and any such conduct is prohibited. The university also prohibits any form of discipline or retaliation for reporting incidents of discrimination.*

- How do the Benedictine values of the University of Mary align with your personal values? Which of these values resonate most deeply with you? Give an example or two.

The written response should reach the University of Mary prior to the time of the interview.

Those applying for positions on the teaching faculty or for senior administrative positions (including—but not limited to—dean, director of athletics, vice president, president) are also expected to read and be conversant in the following two documents:

- *Education within the Benedictine Wisdom Tradition*: This statement of the Association of Benedictine Colleges and Universities sets forth the history and context for Benedictine higher education and enumerates ten "hallmarks" of Benedictine education which complement the university's own six Benedictine values. There is a link to the document at www.umary.edu/hr.
- *Ex corde Ecclesiae*: This apostolic constitution of Pope John Paul II elucidates a Catholic university's responsibilities in the service of truth and the common good, the importance of academic freedom and institutional autonomy, and the nature of the university's relationship with the universal Church. *Ex corde Ecclesiae* constitutes one of the University of Mary's governing documents. There is a link to the document at www.umary.edu/hr.

At the discretion of the unit supervisor, applicants for certain director-level positions may also be asked to consider these two documents in their preparation.

## Interview with the University President

Finalists in the interview process are scheduled for a personal meeting with the university president, after which time a hiring decision will be made. Unless special arrangements have been made, application materials should reach the office of the president at least two days prior to this meeting.

Reviewed and approved by University Legal Counsel, 11 January 2011
Approved by the President's Council, 12 January 2011

*Timothy Seaworth is Vice President for Student Development at University of Mary, Bismarck, ND.*

*We extend our gratitude to Father Shea and the University of Mary for graciously sharing their hiring-for-mission process with us and allowing us to print their "Hiring for Mission at the University of Mary" document.*

## chapter TWENTY-NINE

## Lewis University's Hiring for Mission Program

*Lewis University*

Lewis University's commitment to its Catholic and Lasallian mission is demonstrated in a variety of ways. One such expression of this is the "Hiring for Mission" program. *Hiring for Mission is the process by which Lewis University informs candidates about its Catholic and Lasallian mission and makes "commitment to advancing the mission" one of the key elements of the hiring process.* In mission-based hiring, the best-qualified candidate is the person who exhibits competency for the position and has the desired qualifications, but it is someone who also demonstrates appreciation for and understanding of our Catholic and Lasallian identity, as well as expresses a commitment to advancing the mission.

Formally launched in 1999, this program has been refined and enhanced over the course of the past fourteen years. Although all those who participate in the hiring of new faculty and staff members play a critical role in making this effort successful, the Hiring for Mission program is carefully coordinated by staff in the Office of Mission and Identity and in the Office of Human Resources.

### The Hiring for Mission Process

- All potential employees learn about the mission of Lewis University through announcements of open positions that reference the Catholic and Lasallian nature of the institution. These announcements are both web-based and in print.
- Interested individuals complete an online application and as part of this process are required to verify that they have read the university's mission statement (www.lewisu.edu/mission).
- During phone and on-campus interviews, hiring managers or search committee members create a dialogue with the candidate about the mission, and discuss how they relate to it, and will advance it, if hired. (Hiring managers have a list of sample questions and prompts, as well as a list of what to listen for during the interviews.) Finalists visit campus to spend time interviewing with a variety of individuals, meet students, and participate in "open sessions" with faculty and staff. Dialogue around mission continues to occur during this part of the process.
- All finalists receive a follow-up e-mail from the Office of Human Resources that includes the link to a web-based *Hiring for Mission Response Form* (http://www.

lewisu.edu/missionresponseform/), which candidates are asked to complete within twenty-four hours of visiting campus. The form includes the following question:

> *If hired, how will you advance the mission of Lewis University in the position for which you are applying?*

When the candidate submits the response to this question, it is reviewed by the Director or Human Resources and the Vice President for Mission and Academic Services. This brief essay then becomes part of the candidate's application materials and can be referenced throughout the hiring process.

- Once the search committee has made its decision and final recommendation, the hiring manager must write a brief paragraph-long *Hiring Manager's Mission Endorsement* of the candidate that attests to his or her "mission fit." The hiring manager responds to this prompt:

> *I recommend that the above named candidate be employed at Lewis University. The candidate demonstrates an ability to advance and contribute to the mission in the following manner:*

The hiring manager may cite examples from the interview process or from the candidate's *Hiring for Mission Response Form* in this formal endorsement of the candidate. The endorsement is about two paragraphs in length.

- The finalist's *Hiring for Mission Response Form* and the *Hiring Manager's Mission Endorsement*, along with other pertinent materials are then reviewed by the appropriate dean or vice president/provost as well as by the president and then a final decision is made.

- New employees participate in a one-on-one or small group mission orientation meeting and then meet with the president of the university to be formally presented with an appointment letter. All new employees are also required to participate in a daylong *New Employee Mission Orientation Workshop, Commissioning Service and Welcoming Luncheon* program in January or August.

## Hiring for Mission Training Workshops for Hiring Managers

Hiring for Mission training workshops are required for all hiring managers and are held periodically or on an "as-needed" basis. The objective of these workshops is to discuss the importance of Hiring for Mission and to provide an overview of the complete Hiring for Mission process described above. Led by a team of administrators from the Office of Mission and Identity and the Office of Human Resources, these workshops begin with a formal address by the president of the university, who emphasizes the importance of mission-based hiring and references important foundational documents, such as *Ex corde Ecclesiae*, the university's mission statement, and the sponsorship covenant of the De La Salle Christian Brothers.

The workshop also features hands-on exercises that help hiring managers: (1) assess appropriate kinds of mission-inspired interview questions and create a dialogue around mission during the interview; (2) assess mission fit during the interview and in review of the *Hiring for Mission Response Forms*; and (3) write the *Hiring Manager's Mission Endorsement*.

The workshops also provide an opportunity for hiring managers to explore best practices, share experiences, and ask questions concerning the hiring process. Above all, the workshop instills confidence in hiring managers and affirms their very important role in promoting and advancing Lewis University's Catholic and Lasallian identity through our hiring practices.

There are approximately one hundred seventy formally designated hiring managers at Lewis University – these individuals include members of the administration, as well as directors, academic department chairs, and program coordinators. During the fall of 2012 and spring of 2013, one hundred forty of these hiring managers (eighty-two percent of those formally designated) participated in one of the four *Hiring for Mission* workshops.

*We extend our gratitude to Brother James Gaffney and Lewis University for graciously allowing us to print their hiring for mission document, "Lewis University's Hiring for Mission Program."*

# section Six
●●●●●●

**Spirituality, Ecumenical, and Interfaith Issues on Campus**

## chapter THIRTY

## The Role of the Mission Officer in Encouraging Spirituality within the Mercy Tradition

*Jean Roche, RSM*

Unprecedented change appears to be the hallmark of society today. In many spheres of human endeavor, systems and institutions that served well in the past are no longer adequate to support emerging thought and innovation. Housten (2000) states: "We need a spiritual renaissance commensurate with our technological developments to give us a sufficiency of inner inspiration to guide our expanding outer forms" (p. 15). A spiritual perspective is needed to ground, inspire, and heal the human community. This article will address the role of the mission officer as an "animator of spirituality" and provide practical examples in three topic areas: facilitating the discovery of a spiritual identity, modeling inclusivity, and creating sacred space.

Over the years the Institute Leadership Team of the Sisters of Mercy of the Americas has emphasized the fact that higher education requires a commitment to the spiritual well-being of the human community.

● ● ● ● ● ● ● ● ● ● ● ● ● ● ● ● ● ● ● ● ● ● ● ● ● ● ● ● ● ●

### Mission Officer as Animator

The role of the mission officer is not only that of imparting information; it is also one of animation—bringing to life, inspiring, evoking creativity and joy. Indeed, the foundress of the Sisters of Mercy according to biographers Regan and Keiss (1998) stated that "the primary role of the leader is animator" (p. 69). One mission officer acted as an animator when she created a fourteen-member Mission Animation Team representing a cross section of the college community. The primary goal of this committee was to raise consciousness of the mission of mercy, not only through the dissemination of information but also through engagement. Rather than impose a set of values determined by a senior administrative body, the team engaged the entire community of administrators, students, faculty, and staff in a discernment process. Each had the opportunity to express views regarding the most salient values of the institution flowing from its mission statement. Interviews conducted by the mission officer and campus minister served to raise consciousness and stimulate interest in the project. This process included the identification and promulgation of the core values of compassion, service, community, integrity, respect, and scholarship. A similar process, relative to the creation of a vision statement, included creating and displaying vision boards in key locations of the campus as a way of tilling the soil of imagination as the process continued. Another simple yet energizing activity involved having members of the college community write on sticky pads those things they deemed especially meaningful and memorable about the institution. The results, which were displayed throughout the campus on large posters, generated enthusiastic conversations, as well as moments of thoughtful reflection.

One of the most successful and animated Spring Mission Awareness Days was conceived by the mission officer and team. Each department was challenged to create an experience relative to mission and core values for the entire college community. This endeavor evoked the energy, talents, and enthusiasm of both leaders and students throughout the campus.

The Early Childhood Department displayed colorful core value posters and invited participants to sign a pledge of commitment to a specific action. Occupational therapy students guided participants in the creation of a mission and core values quilt. Nursing students designed a ritual to avoid burnout. The Bereavement Studies Department distributed a newsletter demonstrating how graduates were utilizing their training through formal and informal service-learning in churches, synagogues, hospices, prisons, addiction centers, schools, and centers for the homeless. A meditation on mercy was created and distributed by the campus minister. The English Department gave instructions on writing a haiku related to the mission of mercy. This experience blossomed as students began to write haikus for their instructors and one another.

## Discovering Spiritual Identity

The mission officer is gifted with the opportunity to bring together members of the campus for spiritual growth. The creation of a heterogeneous spirituality group involving students and faculty of diverse religious and spiritual traditions can reveal surprising commonalities. Inviting students to write and share a personal creed based on "an inner knowing," rather than the rote recitation of a prescribed religious formula, often proves to be a unifying experience. The use of an instrument such as *Who Is My God? An Innovative Guide to Finding Your Spiritual Identity* (Skylight Paths, 2000) can be enlightening in terms of one's own beliefs as well as those of others, as can exposing students to the prayers inherent in diverse cultures through books such as *Prayers for Healing* (Oman, 1999). Other resources such as *Earth Prayers* (Roberts & Amidon, 1991) and *Life Prayers* (Robert & Amidon, 1996) can reveal considerable congruence with the Christian belief system.

## Inclusivity

While an emphasis on the social teaching of the Catholic Church and identification with the healing mission of Jesus is paramount, it is important to be wary of reductionism and remain mindful of the richness inherent in the diverse religious and spiritual traditions on multicultural campuses. It is no secret that there are dozens of different spiritual traditions followed in America today, from Buddhism to Roman Catholicism, from Sufism to New Consciousness spirituality. Such diversity is increasingly prevalent on the college campus. Consequently, it would be wise for mission officers to be guided by the wisdom of the mystic Mechtild who wrote: "How shall we live? Live welcoming to all" (Woodruff, 1982, p. 126). Such is the notion of hospitality inherent in most mainstream religious traditions.

Inclusivity of those who belong to other faith traditions, as well as those who profess no religious belief at all, can be fostered by the creation of prayer services and rituals on universal themes of love, peace, forgiveness, mercy, and justice. Various media can be utilized including poetry, music, guided meditation, storytelling, expressive art, and symbolic action. Another means of inclusion is the creation of spiritual support groups. Seeds for the creation of action-oriented prayer services may be found in the book *Praying with Catherine McAuley* (Burns & Carney, 1996). Rooted in the Gospel and the Mercy charism, the book also has universality in term of themes, reflection, and specific suggestions for ameliorative action. A simple international potluck luncheon, inviting participants to bring a cultural culinary contribution, can provide an excellent beginning for group sharing.

## Creating Sacred Space

Most Catholic universities have a chapel, which provides sacred space and serves as a gathering place for the community. One cannot overestimate the spiritual power inherent in the Gospel values and in the healing mission of Jesus. The offices of the mission officer and campus minister can model an atmosphere of peace, joy, and positive energy. A fountain of flowing water, live plants, soft music, and photographs or paintings reflecting the beauty of creation can provide a relaxing space for reflection and refreshment. A mission officer's library of traditional, mystical, and spiritual books needs to be updated regularly.

Maria College, on the site of a former Dominican monastery, is especially blessed with sacred space, including a "monastery garden" with a fountain and a student lounge featuring a large stained glass window, as well as traditional prayer stalls and contemporary furniture.

Catholic identity also enhances beauty on the campus through meaningful liturgical celebrations, colorful vestments, and sacred symbols. The sacramental life of the Church fosters community, reconciliation, healing, and peace. Ecclesiastical advocacy regarding social justice issues provides the impetus to action and service-learning opportunities among the poor and vulnerable, including children, women, and the elderly.

## Conclusion

The mission officer of the contemporary college campus has countless opportunities to be an instrument of life and growth with respect to mission, core values, spirituality, and service. It is by no means a solitary task, but rather one that demands the energy and engagement of each member of the college community. In order to fulfill the goal of integration, the mission officer needs to partner with persons representative of a cross section of the college community in a working relationship. Collaboration with the campus minister is essential. The arena of education today, perhaps even more than the Church, is the most fertile soil for the education and healing of many students. The mission officer, by offering an array of spirituality experiences, can make a significant difference in the lives of the members of the university community for many years to come.

*Sr. Jean Roche, RSM recently retired as Campus Minister, and Bereavement Studies Coordinator and Mission Animation Coordinator at Maria College, Albany, NY.*

---

*References*

Housten, J. (2000). *Jump Time.* New York, NY: Jeremy Tarcher.

Regan, J. & I. Keiss. (1988). *Tender Courage.* Chicago, IL: Franciscan Herald Press.

Woodruff, S. (1982). *Meditations with Mechtild.* Santa Fe, NM: Bear & Company, Inc.

## chapter THIRTY-ONE

## That All May Be One: Ecumenism and a Catholic College or University

*Helen Marie Burns, RSM*

One task of Catholic higher education is to provide a context where people can search together for understanding and insight regarding meaning in the world in which they live. Campus ministers and mission officers focus this task through the lens of faith, spirituality, and moral choices. In an era in which the world has become divisive and proclamations of faith-based positions tend toward rhetorical and real violence, the effort to understand other believers within the Christian family and to engage them in respectful and civil dialogue is essential. Ecumenism, the movement toward unity or cooperation among the Christian churches, is an important element of both campus ministry and mission work. Interfaith dialogue, that is conversation among and between different faith traditions, is equally important, but not the topic or the focus of this article.

> "A Catholic University...is immersed in human society; as an extension of its service to the Church, and always within its proper competence, it is called on to become an ever more effective instrument of cultural progress for individuals as well as for society." (Ex corde Ecclesiae, 32)

While Catholic higher education offers an important venue in which diverse experiences, creeds, and theologies may meet in valuable exchange and exploration, the potential for each institution's engagement in ecumenism must be examined. Then, responses can be developed that honor the story and tradition of sponsoring bodies, as well as the geographic and intellectual location of the institution.

### Geography, Regional Culture, and Religious Diversity Make a Difference

Mount Aloysius College offers a case study. Its unique characteristics are noted here only to pattern the analysis that each institution, through its mission officer, must undertake. The college is located in rural, western Pennsylvania. The religious profile of the area is predominantly Christian, but not Roman Catholic. (The *Mount Aloysius College 2011 Fact Book* indicated that 478 of 1,692 students did not answer a question concerning religious affiliation, and 1 percent indicated no preference or affiliation.) Enrollment of Catholic students has been trending downward—from a majority of 54 percent a decade ago to 39 percent recently. Still, the Catholic cohort is the largest specific church affiliation on campus.

Mount Aloysius is sponsored by the Sisters of Mercy whose foundress, Catherine McAuley, lived and died in nineteenth-century Ireland in a time of much religious prejudice. Early Sisters of Mercy in the United States were victims of more than one convent-burning by anti-Catholic movements. Openness to various Christian churches and awareness of religious differences marks the story of the Sisters of Mercy from the diverse Christian influences (Catholic, Quaker, and Anglican, especially) on Catherine herself, to works of education and healthcare, which incorporated sensitivity to a variety of Christian believers.

This Mercy story converged in the twenty-first century with a generous donation to the college by a local Lutheran pastor, Gerald L. Myers. In April 2000, Pastor Myers donated his personal theological library to the college to provide "the people of Allegheny region with a resource that could be used by all denominations." That donation formed the core of an Ecumenical Studies Collection that now consists of more than 17,570 volumes mainly in the fields of theology, religion, philosophy, Old and New Testament studies, ethics, religious art and music, Christian spirituality, feminist theology, Marian studies, ministry, and pastoral care. That donation, along with a growing religious diversity on the campus, also led to a deliberate focus on ecumenism which marks the work of the mission officer and campus ministers.

### Collaboration with the Leaders of Other Areas of the Campus is Essential

Collaboration in planning and programming among and between the mission officer and campus minister provides an opportunity to balance the demands of Catholic identity and the demands of ecumenical awareness and outreach. Each office needs to identify in its planning process those activities and programs that will address the needs of Catholic students and the needs of other Christian churches, and to determine which office will take the lead in execution. In the instance of Mount Aloysius College, the mission officer oversees campus ministry, the Ecumenical Studies Center, and the Community Engagement and Social Entrepreneurship Center, so annual planning occurs together and provides an opportunity for coordination and collaboration. Ecumenical activities and programs have been allocated in the following manner:

| Campus Ministry | Mission Office |
|---|---|
| +Orientation (students) | +Orientation (parents/employees) |
| +Catholic worship services | +Christian Unity Service |
| +Thanksgiving ecumenical service | +Moral Choices Lecture |
| +Ecumenical Bible studies | +Ecumenical luncheon/lecture |
| +Busy Persons Retreat (ecumenical leaders) | +Summer Scripture Institute |

Opportunities for collaboration are many, limited only by time and by energy. Campus ministry can host a resource table during orientation that introduces their staff as resources for all persons interested in faith development and spiritual growth. Handouts announcing time and place of Catholic liturgies might also identify local churches of various denominations and the times of their services. Campus ministry can offer to arrange transportation to any of these services for students who might not have access to a car. Likewise, the mission officer can introduce faculty and staff in employee orientation programs to the Catholic identity of the college or university, as well as its ecumenical sensitivity.

A Faith Fair, early in the semester, is also an ideal way to welcome faith leaders to one's campus and to introduce these leaders to the campus community. In the instance of Mount Aloysius College, the Fair is a collaborative venture planned by the Campus Ministry Office and resourced by contacts from the Ecumenical Studies Center.

## Each Campus Community Has Traditions That Lend Themselves to Ecumenical Celebrations

Two major celebrations offer an opportunity for appropriate inclusion of a variety of church leaders in all-campus prayer services: Thanksgiving and the Week of Christian Unity. The campus minister can plan and execute the Ecumenical Thanksgiving Service, while the mission officer might be responsible for the Christian Unity Service. In either case, invitations can happen in a variety of ways: a local minister might be invited to create and preside at a service, or the service might be designed by campus personnel but presided over by a local minister. The selection of hymns and prayers should be sensitive to the various religious affiliations within the campus community. Minimally, the Thanksgiving Prayer Service and Christian Unity Service could feature a sermon by a local church leader.

Smaller efforts to respect ecumenical interests can occur in the area of Scripture Studies and retreat experiences. Facilitation of gatherings to study Scripture might be led by organized Christian groups (e.g., Campus Crusade) or led by students from within a particular Christian denomination (e.g., students who are Mennonite or Disciples of Christ). If the study is led by an organized Christian group, a prior discussion with the leaders needs to establish the ground rules for biblical discussions on a Catholic campus (e.g., anti-Catholic interpretations of the Scriptures need to be avoided, as well as overt use of the Scriptures to denigrate or denounce any particular members of the campus community). Similarly, all retreat experiences sponsored by campus ministers or mission officers should include spiritual companions from a variety of Christian churches or, minimally, persons who are knowledgeable and respectful of this diversity.

## The Catholic University Is Called to Serve the Wider Christian Community

While the fundamental appropriateness and consonance of ecumenical work with Catholic identity and Christian witness is beyond question, the choice to involve the college or university in ecumenical work within the broader community is a decision based on time, personnel, and finances as well as identity. Multiple options are available in terms of this broader involvement: participation in local ecumenical coalitions, programming toward an ecumenical audience, and initiatives that support and enhance local ecumenical activities.

Since the mission which any mission officer shepherds is primarily higher education within a Catholic and, for some institutions, religious congregational framework, the development of an educational outreach which serves the needs of church leaders is most appropriate. Some campuses sponsor ecumenical lecture series, which bring prominent speakers from various Christian denominations to the region. Likewise, an ecumenical luncheon series and/or annual prayer breakfast could provide an opportunity to build community among and between church leaders, and allow them to share input in a manner that builds understanding and knowledge. The college or university might utilize its communication resources to publish a newsletter highlighting ecumenical happenings among and between the churches. Programming summer events with a deliberate focus on the need for continuing education of church leaders (pastors, youth leaders, adult educators, etc.) presents a win-win situation in which campus resources are engaged and local needs are addressed.

Mount Aloysius College held a yearlong exploration on "The Role of the University in Civil Discourse," which was published as a monograph and can be retrieved through the Library of Congress at: http://www.mtaloy.edu/about_mac/news_events/news_detail.dot?inode=1311417&crumbTitle=News%20Detail.

## Conclusion

Clearly the documents of the Second Vatican Council, the more recent publication of *Ex corde Ecclesiae,* and the ongoing work of the Pontifical Commission for Church Unity signal the importance of ecumenism to our identity as Catholic and to our living witness of Gospel values. The unfulfilled prayer of Jesus, "that they may all be one; even as You, Father, are in Me and I in You, that they also may be in Us, so that the world may believe that You sent Me" (John 17:21) impels faithful persons to prayer and to action. Faithful institutions of higher education "immersed in human society …and…called…to become an ever more effective instrument of cultural progress…for society" (*Ex corde Ecclesiae*, 32) need to commit themselves to prayer and to action and to understand themselves as vibrant centers of ecumenical engagement.

*Sr. Helen Marie Burns, RSM, is Vice President of Mission Integration at Mount Aloysius College, Cresson, PA.*

## chapter THIRTY-TWO

## Interfaith and Ecumenical Engagement: The Terrain of the Church

*James Puglisi*

A religiously diverse population on a Catholic campus is not the imperative for addressing religious diversity; it is because the campus *is* Catholic that there is an imperative to address interfaith and ecumenical engagement.

Religious diversity in Catholic higher education poses both challenges and opportunities in fostering a rich Catholic environment. Despite possible perceptions that fostering Catholic identity might be at odds with cultivating religious diversity, the Church has been an engaged interfaith and ecumenical dialogue partner, specifically as articulated in Vatican II documents, in the writings and work of Pope John Paul II (Gioia, 2006), and more recently with Pope Francis. Pope Francis affirms the importance of interfaith engagement, asserting that "every man is the image of God, whether he is a believer or not" (Bergoglio, p. 13). The search for truth, wherever it is found, is consistent with the Catholic Intellectual Tradition. The precedence for interfaith and ecumenical work is in place through various Church documents and papal writings (www.vatican.va); but what is the *mission* imperative for addressing religious pluralism on the Catholic campus?

Familiarity with the Church's teaching provides a platform from which to envision what a campus might cultivate in support of its religious diversity. At the core of Catholic higher education is the search for truth, wherever it is expressed (*Ex corde Ecclesiae*, 1). Religiously diverse students and parents often prefer Catholic institutions specifically because of the institution's freedom to address issues of religion and faith in the search for truth, which are not always permitted within public colleges and universities. The ability to view the Catholic Church through the historical and contextual lens of those whose experience is outside of the Church will assist in building bridges of trust and acceptance. History shows that there have been tensions between religious traditions for various reasons, some of which

The Interfaith Youth Corp (ifyc.org) and Catholic Association of Diocesan Ecumenical and Interreligious Officers (cadeio.org) offer practical resources for developing interfaith and ecumenical practices. The Offices of Mission and Values at DePaul University and Dominican University offer examples of approaching religious diversity within a large Catholic urban institution and a smaller Catholic suburban institution.

fall outside the realm of religious belief. It is necessary neither to downplay, nor to highlight these historical tensions. It is prudent to be aware of events in history and culture that might directly or indirectly impact the community in its particular context. People look for a school or work environment that is accepting and nurturing. They are rarely interested in resolving historical issues of tension. As campus communities become increasingly more religiously and culturally diverse, knowledge of the global reach of the Church can be beneficial, particularly where Christianity is a minority religious tradition.

## What Can Be Done On Campus?

The building of personal relationships is the core of any interfaith and ecumenical initiative. These relationships will help to create a community of inquiry and friendship, while campus norms and operating practices are impacted by the increasing presence of religious diversity. There are tools and processes that may be helpful:

1. *Focus on Local Issues and Relationships.* Local interfaith and ecumenical partners and initiatives can serve as a resource for the institution. Familiarity with both official and informal dialogues between various religious traditions and denominations is not vital. However, it would be wise to have knowledge of their existence, because they set the precedents for interfaith and ecumenical engagement. Explore the interfaith and ecumenical history of the local diocese and bishop to identify existing pastoral efforts as well as any politically charged tension points. An example of a beneficial ecumenical relationship was the annual meeting of Christian Churches Together, hosted by the Diocese of Austin, Texas, in 2013. This ecumenical gathering produced a Statement of Intent regarding baptism between several denominations as well as the adoption of a statement calling for fundamental immigration reform, an issue of importance for Roman Catholics in central Texas.

2. *Know the Campus Context.* Campuses change consistently, and institutional memory is often limited to the tenure of the current population. Review campus archives, old student newspapers, alumni records, and yearbooks to identify alumni and former student groups from diverse religious traditions. Creating an institutional memory could help identify potential alumni advocates and foster acceptance of religious diversity.

3. *Utilize the Charism and History of the Founding Order.* Utilizing the charism and teachings of the founding religious community may provide a template and language in which to foster institutional identity grounded in Catholic identity, while embracing a religious pluralism on campus. An example might be promoting and marketing interfaith and ecumenical events, or utilizing quotations from writings of the founding order that promote the acceptance and need for religious pluralism.

4. *Foster Collaboration between the Campus and Community Partners and Advocates.* Foster allies within the local community through religious and cultural associations. Most urban centers have various interfaith bodies that engage community issues and can be a valuable resource. Smaller communities may have ecumenical ministerial bodies comprised of mainline Protestant ministers open to religious pluralism.

Local partners may provide resources for the campus community and serve as advocates with other community religious organizations in the case of religiously negative on-campus situations. Look beyond the Religious Studies department for on-campus partners. There is often a fine line between cultural and religious diversity. Offices working with multiculturalism, international students, retention issues, orientation, faculty development in teaching diverse populations, student housing, study-abroad, as well as other offices all deal with issues related to religious diversity. The community needs to suggest ways to show respect for religious and cultural diversity. Small steps can make a difference. Perhaps the dining service could provide a halal option for Muslim students on Fridays. Would the university community consider providing prayer space for Muslims, or allowing a Muslim chaplain?

5.  *Be Aware of Christian Diversity and Embrace It.* Be mindful of differences in mainline, evangelical, and fundamentalist Christian bodies and denominations, as well as the growing presence of non-denominational churches. Christian pluralism should be respected, particularly in the current polarized political climate. Many campuses have created environments that are more open to interfaith diversity than they are to ecumenical diversity and the divergent views of the faith within Christianity. Meet with ecumenical leaders and pastors from local churches that serve students, or participate in Christian Unity Week which is celebrated internationally each January. This is an excellent opportunity to work with students from across the Christian spectrum.

6.  *Mission Statements and Operating Principles Are Important.* Institutional mission statements should reflect a commitment to cultural and religious diversity. Where not explicitly named, it should be a stated priority. Any presentation of the institution's Mission and Identity should articulate the purpose and desired outcome of developing a Catholic identity that draws upon the full font of the Church's knowledge and teaching, which includes engaging religious diversity. The Second Vatican Council itself was an ecumenical council and the imperative for interreligious engagement is offered in the Vatican II document, *Nostra Aetate*: "The Church…exhorts her sons, that through dialogue and collaboration with the followers of other religions…in witness to the Christian faith and life… (to) recognize, preserve and promote the good things, spiritual and moral, as well as the socio-cultural values found among these men" (2). The presence of a religiously diverse population will naturally raise questions about differences that exist. To adequately respond to these questions, an institution must gain clarity regarding core beliefs and mission. Mission and Identity content should be grounded in the magisterial teachings (Gioia, 2006), drawing upon other related resources (Patel, 2008 & 2012, Heckman, 2008), and presented in an accessible manner. This is a catechetical moment for all.

7.  *Religious Inclusivity Is Not Religious Relativism.* Initiatives in support of religious diversity must enhance Catholic identity. Mere "accommodation" falls short. Religiously diverse students know, often more so than Catholic students, that they

are entering a Catholic environment. An institution should not hide its Catholic identity. It can provide an atmosphere that includes all faiths. Pope John Paul II offered the prayer at the Assisi World Day of Prayer for Peace, "as a visible illustration, a lesson of facts, a catechism intelligible to all, of what the ecumenical commitment and the commitment for interreligious dialogue presuppose can signify." Avoid speaking for other faiths and praying in the "we" if invoking Christ at religiously diverse gatherings. Be aware of the choice of pronouns used. One way to enrich the prayer life and spirituality of all concerned is to rotate the prayer leader among the diverse religious groups on campus.

8. *Establish a Common Language for the Institution.* An essential tool in fostering the interfaith and ecumenical presence is language. Sadly, much of the language associated with religion in the media is the "language of domination" (Patel, 2012, p. 140). Traditional Catholic language in campus publications and public addresses may be an unintentional barrier in creating a religiously welcoming community. Words and phrases such as *Mass, liturgy, adoration, Eucharist, pre/post-Vatican II, Catholic Social Teaching, Mass of the Holy Spirit,* and *new evangelism* may be met with a blank face. The latter might even suggest a desire to convert the individual. Images, another form of language, are also contextual and rooted in the culture of the Church with metaphors and meanings that are often controversial or not self-evident. What a wonderful *catechetical* opportunity! For example, a glossary that identifies terms, images, and phrases germane to the campus, religious order, and tradition could be prepared and distributed to students and staff. It could also include key terms from non-Catholic faiths represented on campus.

> St. Edward's University developed a glossary originating out of the Office of Residence Life and later adopted for the Division of Student Affairs. The glossary defines words, phrases, and symbols within Catholicism and the founding order of which the larger community may be unaware.

9. *Create an Environment That Honors the Spirituality of All Employees.* The Catholic institution's purpose is a student-centered endeavor. Yet it is also a place of employment, which functions like other businesses regarding staffing issues and policies that reflect a Judeo-Christian framework. The mission officer can create safe spaces of dialogue in which issues related to religious diversity can be raised without the fear of employment backlash. Establishing policies broad enough to fit all needs is improbable,

> Campus Ministry at St. Edward's University collaborates with the campus Jewish student organization and local Jewish community to annually host a Passover Seder meal. The Seder provides a worship opportunity for the campus' Jewish community, but is open to all members of the campus community.

but the institution can clearly express that there is room to consider individual diverse situations for both employees and students. For example, the Student Affairs Division at St. Edward's University offers a monthly forum entitled "Difficult Dialogues" addressing topics of concern brought forth by staff in the division related to the field of student affairs within a Catholic setting.

10. *It is Both an Academic Exercise and a Religious Experience.* The study of a tradition and the lived experience within a tradition are very different realities. Foster an environment that allows for the exploration of culture while respecting the religious observances that may be taking place simultaneously. For example, the annual Campus Passover Seder offers a great portal into Jewish culture and belief systems: yet, for Jewish attendants, this is a ritual expression of their faith and must be respected as such.

## Conclusion

Catechizing an institution's Catholic population to understand that interfaith and ecumenical engagement is an integral part of the work of the Church is an essential task of Catholic higher education. Addressing and working against a history of real and often perceived tension between the Church and other faith traditions opens the door to forgiveness and reconciliation among all God's children. Engaging a dialogical approach offers a rich opportunity for both global awareness and the fostering of a Catholic identity that is intellectually formed and culturally relevant.

*James Puglisi is Associate Director of Campus Ministry and an Adjunct Faculty in University Programs at St. Edward's University, Austin, TX.*

*References*

Bergoglio, Jorge Mario and Abraham Skorka. (2010). *On Heaven and Earth.* Trans. Alejandro Bermudez and Howard Goodman, ed. in Spanish, Diego F. Rosemberg. New York, NY: Image Books.

Gioia, Francesco, ed. (2006). *Interreligious Dialogue: The Official Teaching of the Catholic Church from the Second Vatican Council to John Paul II (1963-2003).* Boston, MA: Pauline Books & Media.

Heckman, Bud and Rori Picker Neiss, eds. (2008). *Interactive Faith: The Essential Interreligious Community-Building Handbook.* Woodstock, VT: Skylight Paths Publishing.

Nostra Aetate (1965). http://www.vatican.va/archive/hist_councils/ii_vatican_council/documents/vat-ii_decl_19651028_nostra-aetate_en.html.

Patel, Eboo. (2012). *Sacred Ground: Pluralism, prejudice and the promise of America.* Boston, MA: Beacon Press.

Patel, Eboo and Patrice Brodeur, eds. (2006). *Building the Interfaith Youth Movement.* Lanham, MD: Rowman & Littlefield.

*Additional Resources:*

Catholic Association of Diocesan Ecumenical and Interreligious Officers. *http://cadeio. org.*

Pontifical Council for Inter-religious Dialogue. http://www.vatican.va/roman_curia/ pontifical_councils/interelg/index.htm.

Office of Ecumenical and Interreligious Affairs. http://www.usccb.org/beliefs-and-teachings/ecumenical-and-interreligious/index.cfm.

## chapter THIRTY-THREE

### Interfaith Relationships

*John Crossin, OSFS*

## Background

The key to interfaith relationships is mutual respect. To come to this respect Catholics must take the time to get to know others personally. These others will be faculty, students, and administrators of the institution itself and Jewish, Muslim, Hindu, and other religious leaders in the community and afar. As the United States becomes more diverse and the countries of the world become more connected, mission officers, students, and faculty will have more opportunities to build relationships with those of other religious faiths. Through such relationships, people not only can come to mutual understanding, but also can pursue the common good of society.

Building and maintaining relationships requires intentional, consistent effort. Experience teaches that it is best to listen first. Listening with head and heart will often encourage others to share significant things about themselves. The mission officer also needs to be open about who he or she is and about her faith and thus model mutual respect in building relationships.

The Secretariat for Ecumenical and Interreligious Affairs offers a monthly online newsletter, which features press releases, video resources, updates on the bishops' ecumenical and interreligious dialogues, and event reminders. Sign up for the SEIA monthly e-newsletter at http://www.usccb.org/beliefs-and-teachings/ecumenical-and-interreligious/seia-newsletter.cfm.

The SEIA frequently updates a video playlist which can be seen at http://www.usccb.org/about/ecumenical-and-interreligious-affairs/videos.cfm.

From honest mutual exchange, relationships can grow. As with Protestant, Orthodox, Anglican, and other fellow Christians, some individuals are more open to relationships than others. Many are quite welcoming, others more distant or reserved. With those who are distant, it is best to keep the doors open. Misunderstandings, bad past experiences, and the anger that goes with them can inhibit relationships. A little gentleness and kindness can open doors that seem closed.

A prayerful review of Church teaching on interfaith relationships can be a good way to prepare for having interfaith conversations. These teachings can easily be found in the

Second Vatican Council's *Declaration on the Relation of the Church to Non-Christian Religions*—often referred to by its Latin title, *Nostra Aetate*. This document is short and powerful. It sets the tone for positive relationships. Subsequent Church documents can be found on the Vatican website www.vatican.va in the section for the Pontifical Council for Interreligious Dialogue.

Interreligious conversations, often referred to more formally as dialogues, usually occur in four interrelated arenas: experience, common work, theology, and spirituality. People often begin by sharing similar experiences, for example life on campus and its benefits. A second arena would be discussing work both parties share, such as common projects and works of charity. Another area would be sharing reflections about theological topics of mutual interest. Finally, a spiritual sharing of how God has spoken in one's life and led one's spiritual journey can deepen friendship. A common perception is that dialogue partners compromise a person's faith. More frequently, the opposite is true. Dialogue forces one to go deeper into his or her faith. Friends from other religions ask questions. Answering them requires reviewing one's understanding of Catholicism. It is possible to move beyond clichés to a richer, more meaningful faith as Catholic beliefs are explained to others.

New understandings of the intersections of faith and mission have been realized by Villanova University faculty from a variety of faith traditions. The Faculty Dialogue Luncheon Program offers regular discussions and promotes critical inquiry among friends who enter into dialogue dedicated to the integration of faith and learning, the hallmark of Augustinian pedagogy. Dialogues begin with ten-minute presentations from three faculty of various departments, faith traditions, and genders.

Friends from other religions are often quite conscientious in their religious practice. This may lead one to strengthen his or her fidelity to prayer. A summer intern at the Secretariat of Ecumenical and Interreligious Affairs of the United States Conference of Catholic Bishops mentioned that she became more serious about attending Mass and praying as she saw the faithfulness of her Muslim friends to their prayers. Faithfulness to religious practice could prove to be a dynamic topic for a campus discussion.

## Practical Suggestions

The goal of interreligious dialogue is deeper mutual understanding and pursuit of the common good of the community. A deeper goal is understanding between peoples and faiths that leads to harmony and peace. As the world becomes more interconnected and migration brings people more into contact with one another, deadly conflicts can ensue. Interfaith understanding helps to build peace.

Here is a non-exhaustive list of practical ways to encourage interfaith understanding:

1. The ongoing building of relationships is essential. Campus populations turn over regularly, and thus a persevering effort is necessary.

2. One or two people can make a difference. If just a couple of people on campus want to conduct a session to promote mutual understanding of Jews and Catholics, for example, encourage them to do so. Experience shows that many

people will participate if a couple of people use their energy and time to organize the meeting. A major effort isn't required.

3.  Encourage prayer and identify appropriate places for prayer on or near campus. These days interreligious prayer is done "in the presence of one another." Prayers are not mixed or said together. Rather, individuals respect the integrity of one another's prayer. Catholics are present in silent support as others pray; Catholics encourage the support of their Muslim, Jewish, and Hindu friends when they are praying.

4.  Bring in a speaker to address or explain one aspect of his or her faith that has wide public interest. This may be the rabbi, imam, or other religious leader of a local congregation, or someone suggested by one of them. Have a respondent to the presentation who will offer a short reflection on the talk given and begin the discussion. The respondent could be a faculty member of the college or university. This facilitates the building of mutual understanding.

5.  Sponsor a "Generations of Faith" day. The Secretariat of Ecumenical and Interreligious Affairs has twice brought together groups of twenty to twenty-five older and (majority) younger Catholics, and members of various other religious traditions, for a day of getting to know one another and learn more about each other. This inexpensive program is easily adaptable to a local campus situation and is described on the Secretariat's website, http://www.usccb.org/beliefs-and-teachings/ecumenical-and-interreligious/, under the Special Events section near the bottom of the left column of information.

6.  Encourage a regular dialogue group or introduce Question and Answer sessions. These might flow out of a lecture, or a "Generations of Faith" day, or from a class offered on campus.

7.  Sponsor an interreligious project that serves the common good. If there is an active interreligious group on campus, members might value taking a Saturday to clean up the local playground or be involved in some hands-on project in the local community.

## Resources

People are the essential resource. One or two people need to be responsible for facilitating interreligious relations on campus. The time required will depend on budget, student population, etc. Learning to build interreligious relationships is part of a student's education in this diverse country and world.

Those responsible will need the virtues of patience and humility. Building relationships, on campus or in the environs, will take time and is an ongoing project. Sometimes mistakes will be made, and the mission officer and others might need to acknowledge ignorance or misperceptions. Relationships built on honesty and humility, however, may last a lifetime.

*Rev. John Crossin, OSFS is Executive Director, Secretariat for Ecumenical and Interreligious Affairs at United States Conference of Catholic Bishops, Washington, DC.*

## chapter THIRTY-FOUR

## Interfaith Prayer Room: A Necessary Space on Catholic Campuses

*Jean Flannelly, SC*

An interfaith prayer room on campus can be an architectural manifestation of the Catholic Intellectual Tradition's commitment to openness and inclusivity, as well as meeting the real needs of students as "emerging adults." The concept of an interfaith prayer room will be explored and a concrete example of one provided.

### Catholic Intellectual Tradition

There are many interpretations of the Catholic Intellectual Tradition, but the search for truth and openness to truth wherever it is to be found are central to its understanding. It is rooted in Incarnation and in the very person of Jesus Christ. One of the implications of the mystery of God entering into human history and "pitching his tent among us" (John 1:14) is that creation is shot through with the divine presence, and human persons have the challenge, privilege, and responsibility of finding God in all things. Jesus' claim, "I am the Way, and the Truth, and the Life" (John 14:6) is to be taken seriously. Jesus' promise that He and the Father would send another Advocate, the Spirit of Truth, who would remind, guide, and complete the mission of Jesus aids in the struggle to understand the length and breadth of this revelation. This conviction that human persons are made for truth and must search it out wherever it is to be found is seen in the early Church, expressed in the writings of the Fathers and Mothers, given vibrant witness in Thomas Aquinas' refinement of the thought of Aristotle and Averroes and, in modern times, articulated in Newman's *Idea of the University*. It follows from this that Catholic higher education, to be true to its intellectual tradition, must provide a welcoming space for other religious traditions which seek to know the Mystery who embraces all and grounds all beings.

Another way of understanding this commitment to inclusivity is grounded in the belief in a Triune God. Too often this basic Christian belief is approached mathematically: one God, three Persons, rather than as Mystery requiring a long, contemplative gaze. The Triune God is a study in relationship, and as such is a model for living out the Catholic identity. The unity of God is not threatened by deep and real Otherness.

### Composition of Student Bodies

Several characteristics of current student bodies help make the case for an interfaith prayer room. Psychological literature recognizes that adolescence or the period of "emerging adults" in the United States now extends to age twenty-five. One of the most important developmental tasks during adolescence is the establishment of personal identity—a process that involves the questioning of inherited beliefs and value systems and choosing the beliefs and values that will guide the adolescent through adulthood. To do this requires quiet space and time for the individual to distance her or himself from the many voices competing for attention, and discern the voice that is and will be authentic. Technology, often described as a mixed blessing, plays a role here. It allows an individual to be connected twenty-four hours a day and seven days a week, to be in instant contact with the global world, and to establish networks of relationships that would have been impossible twenty years ago.

"Silence is God's first language and everything else is a poor translation." (Thomas Keating, *Invitation to Love: The Way of Christian Contemplation*, 1992)

The dark side of being connected twenty-four hours a day and seven days a week is the lack of space and initiative to be quiet and reflective. A challenge, then, is to motivate students to disconnect and find time and space to come to know themselves and reflect on life's bigger questions, rather than settling for somebody else's answers to these

"If we always rush, achieve, grasp, or fill the hours with mindless busy-ness, how shall we hear the still small voice of our loving Creator who is always inviting us to fullness of life?" (Elizabeth Canham, *Heart Whispers*, 1999)

significant questions. In addition, emerging adults are immersed in a cultural reality where relativism rather than truth, self-centeredness rather than otherness, and an amorphous spirituality rather than a specific religious tradition is often championed.

Regardless of an individual's religious upbringing or identity, research has shown that young adults as a whole are striving to bring meaning to their lives. Catholic higher education can help them meet this goal. *Ex corde Ecclesiae* clearly acknowledges that "the university community of many Catholic institutions includes members of other Churches, ecclesial communities and religions, and also those who profess no religious belief" (section II, 26). Indeed, the diversity of faiths present on contemporary Catholic campuses represent just one way in which Catholic higher education demonstrates its inclusiveness.

Today's college students are more diverse than previous generations and very often lacking in knowledge of their own religious traditions. This religious illiteracy is across traditions. CHE are institutions concerned with the growth and transformation of the whole person, therefore psychological and spiritual development is part of the agenda in addition to academics. Catholic higher education is called to a respectful openness and dialogue with ideas and insights that differ from an individual's own in order to come to know the truth that "will make you free" (John 8:32). An interfaith prayer room can help a campus address the need for inclusivity and the need for meditative quiet.

**Interfaith Prayer Room**

An interfaith prayer room should be one that is a welcoming and hospitable space to any and all traditions. These are essential ingredients in facilitating the process of moving inward. The present age and culture recognize a plurality of faith perspectives that attempt to articulate their experience of the transcendent within human experience. Using a contemplative lens to understand the various beliefs, it becomes clearer that, in many instances, it is the same Mystery or reality being articulated, but one's language and assumptions shape what is said and how it is said. There are at least two possible responses to this reality: non-denomination and interfaith. The non-denominational approach recognizes and celebrates the transcendent but, in general, is reluctant to use the signs and symbols of specific religious traditions. The interfaith approach also recognizes and celebrates the transcendent and speaks of this Mystery or reality in the concrete symbols and rituals of the specific religious tradition. In emphasizing the interfaith aspect of the space, opportunities can be provided for individuals to explore, learn, or deepen an understanding of their tradition. Since one of the major functions of any religious tradition is to mediate the presence of God, the failure of an individual to understand her or his tradition deprives her or him of opportunities to encounter the living God.

In addition to providing a quiet, reflective space, the interfaith prayer room can be an ideal place for conducting meditation sessions and ecumenical prayer services.

**An Example of an Interfaith Prayer Room**

Founders Hall at the College of Mount Saint Vincent houses a large chapel dedicated to Mary under the title of the Immaculate Conception. Open twenty-four hours a day and seven days a week, it is used for weekly Eucharistic Liturgies, the Mass of the Holy Spirit, Baccalaureate Mass, and occasional memorial liturgies and prayer services. At times, students, faculty, and staff drop in for prayer. Its size and presence of Roman Catholic symbols speak to many but not all religious traditions. Adjacent to the chapel is a small room that has been converted from an all-purpose meeting room to the prayer room. At the entrance to the prayer room is a sign welcoming all and asking all to respect the silence of the room. The room is carpeted and has a couch, chairs, and pillows. Opposite the entrance are two windows overlooking a soon-to-be landscaped garden. In between the two windows is a tall fountain. The flowing water has a calming and centering effect. The only adornments on the neutral-colored walls are three poster-size photos: a butterfly, a path leading to a distant unknown place, and a water scene with a bridge. The photos evoke a sense of the transcendent. There is a table that eventually will have prayer material from the different traditions represented in the college. The room has a closet, which provides both storage and a place where Muslim students can leave their prayer rugs. Overall the room facilitates quiet, stillness, and invites an inward movement.

## Some Issues to Consider

Committee involvement is important both for input and ownership. Faculty and students representing different religious traditions can develop greater awareness of, and sensitivity to, the practices and symbols of differing traditions. For example, Roman Catholicism, in its sacramentality, is very comfortable with icons and statues, but both Judaism and Islam forbid such representations. Faculty and students invested in the development of the prayer room are ambassadors for its presence and purpose.

During Lent, a five-part series on "Names of God" was held in the prayer room. Using both Hebrew and Christian Scripture, the participants explored their names for and images of God. One of the participants, a Jewish faculty member, enriched the explorations and discussions by reading from the Hebrew Scripture.

• • • • • • • • • • • • • • • • • • • • • • • • • • • • • • • •

The location of the prayer room is another consideration. The choice to locate the room next to the main chapel was directed by practical and symbolic issues. The space next to the chapel was available; more importantly its location underscored the connection between the two sacred spaces.

With many voices competing for attention, it was necessary to get messages out early and often. The formal dedication of the prayer room, a way of calling attention to the existence and purpose of the new initiative, was announced through e-mails and digital signage. Reminders were sent and posted. The dedication ceremony included prayers and reflections from differing faith traditions and an invitation to use the room for quiet and reflection.

## Summary

Catholic higher education is committed to the education of the whole person. Central to the human person is openness to transcendence. The cultural climate in the United States fosters a hunger for the spiritual but lacks the religious language and symbols of the major religious traditions. With a profound respect for differing religious traditions, Catholic higher education is in a privileged position to offer the needed language and symbols. Emerging adults can be, and ought to be, assisted in their spiritual and psychological journey. An interfaith prayer room as described earlier is an invaluable asset in educating the whole person.

*Sr. Jean Flannelly, SC is Executive Director for Mission at the College of Mount Saint Vincent, Riverdale, NY.*

## section SEVEN
● ● ● ● ● ●

**Prayers for Various Occasions**

**Prayer for Welcoming New Faculty and Staff**

*Debra Mooney*


Thank You, O Holy One, for all that has led to this wonderful day. It is with great anticipation, hope, and joy that we greet our new companions. With them, we enter into a most historic period in the life of our university. Bless the wisdom, talents, diversity, and novelty that they bring and share.

For those of us who have called this campus our professional home for years or decades:
- Help us to bring out the best in those we welcome today, as they will bring out the best in us.
- Help us to foster their career endeavors and to be receptive to their fresh ideas.
- Help us to be gracious and supportive guides to those we now call "our new colleagues," but whom we will soon call "our friends."

Together, help us to do Your work by doing our work with excellence and reverence. God bless our shared mission and future.

Amen.


*Debra K. Mooney is the Assistant to the President for Mission & Identity/CMO and Founding Director, Conway Institute for Jesuit Education at Xavier University, Cincinnati, OH.*

## Prayer for the Beginning of the Academic Year (1)

*Sheila Carney, RSM*

God of all our days, of beginnings and endings, we gather this morning on the brink of a new academic year. While we begin anew with fresh energy and renewed hope, we don't know what lies ahead as this year unfolds. What we do know is that *You* are ahead of us, *and* behind us, *and* all around us; and so we are united with confidence that Your loving care continues to surround us.

As we strive to embody the mission of our university, we are grateful for the support, the example, and the encouragement of our co-workers. We celebrate this community and all the ways in which You make Yourself known in its midst.

Amen.

*Sheila Carney, RSM is Special Assistant to the President for Mercy Heritage and Service at Carlow University, Pittsburgh, PA.*

**Prayer for the Beginning of the Academic Year (2)**

*Sheila Carney, RSM*

God, here we are again—faculty and students renewed and eager to begin a new academic year. And here we are still—staff and administration who have worked through the summer to assure that all is ready for this new beginning. While we gather with fresh energy and renewed hope, we don't know what lies ahead as this year unfolds. What we do know is that *You* are ahead of us, *and* behind us, *and* all around us. We are united with confidence that Your loving care continues to surround us as this community once again takes up the challenge of its mission. Be with us as we strive to transform the words we have written into living examples of who and what we have said we will do and be. And let's all say:

Amen.

*Sheila Carney, RSM is Special Assistant to the President for Mercy Heritage and Service at Carlow University, Pittsburgh, PA.*

### Prayer for the Beginning of the Academic Year (3)

*Sheila Carney, RSM*

We gather today in the freshness of a new year. In the midst of the change that newness portends, we remember You, Our God, and Your unchanging fidelity to each of us and to this university. Be with us today as we gather to reflect on this ministry that You have entrusted to our care. Give us ears to hear Your call, give us a sense of common purpose, and give us energy and ingenuity for the work that is ours. In all that we do may our shared effort be to continue to build a university that reflects the mission and values we have espoused. We ask this in the name of Jesus who walked among us as teacher and friend.

Amen.

*Sheila Carney, RSM is Special Assistant to the President for Mercy Heritage and Service at Carlow University, Pittsburgh, PA.*

## Prayer for the Board of Trustees

*Sheila Carney, RSM*

Our God, You have given us responsibility for this campus and for all who work and teach and study here. Help us to take up this responsibility with honesty and integrity, respecting the gifts that each brings to our common endeavor.

Send Your Spirit to be with us in this meeting so that the discussions and decisions that are before us will be infused with the values we proclaim.

We gratefully acknowledge Your presence in our lives and in the life of the university, and we commit ourselves to our continuing search for the deepest meaning of the mission You have entrusted to us. We know that You are with us, as You have been throughout our history, and so we go forward with confidence.

Amen.

*Sheila Carney, RSM is Special Assistant to the President for Mercy Heritage and Service at Carlow University, Pittsburgh, PA.*

## Prayer for Interfaith Gathering

*Carol Ziegler, SND*

Let us bow our heads and recall God's presence within and among us.

God of Abraham and Sarah, God of Isaac and Rebekah, God of Ishmael and daughter, Mahalath, You are Great. Blessed are You for calling us together this evening. We come from courses at the college, a busy day at work or practice, and all the entanglements that are part of life and relating to one another. Our relationships most often are positive, respectful, and energizing. At other times, they can become contentious and difficult because we are unable or unwilling to listen to, understand, or identify with the other.

Tonight, we gather to consider an important topic in our interfaith relationships. We will consider deeply held religious beliefs of people like us, yet, in some deep ways, different from us, whether Muslim, Christian, or Jew.

Each of us stands in confidence and hope looking into the face of the God in whom we believe. As the loving and faithful God of Abraham and Sarah, our commitment to You is holy ground. Tonight open our minds and hearts to understand Your call to the important dialogue around the questions, the prophetic movements among us, and ultimately the call to live as messengers of peace.

Amen.

*Carol Ziegler, SND is Special Assistant for Mission Effectiveness at Notre Dame College, South Euclid, OH.*

## Prayer for the Jesuit Identity Committee of the Board of Trustees

*Debra Mooney*

Good and loving God, we gather this morning in Your name.

The gifts of our _____ heritage invite us to be part of a tradition that builds on the wisdom of the past with a vision open to the opportunities of the future.

Bless this vital work that we do on behalf of students who, through their education, are challenged to make a difference in the world.

Give us the grace to serve You well. Instill in us the humility to discern Your will and the generosity to carry it out.

We ask this in Your name.

Amen.

*Staff of the Center for Mission and Identity, Xavier University, on behalf of Debra K. Mooney, Assistant to the President for Mission & Identity/CMO and Founding Director, Conway Institute for Jesuit Education at Xavier University, Cincinnati, OH.*

### Prayer for a Presidential Search

*Sheila Carney, RSM*

God of all our days, You have called our university community into a season of transition—a time of probing our hopes and expectations and of inviting new leadership. Send Your wise and Holy Spirit to be with us in the process of seeking a new president. May our conversations be honest, our speech courageous and clear, our discernment rooted in the values we espouse. Gift us with the assurance that You, who have been our Good Companion throughout the history of our university, will continue to enfold us in Your Provident care.

Amen.

*Sheila Carney, RSM is Special Assistant to the President for Mercy Heritage and Service at Carlow University, Pittsburgh, PA.*

## Prayer for the State of the University Address

*Sheila Carney, RSM*

We gather in this day, our God, to reflect on the life of our university, on its vitality, on its blessings and shortcomings, on the fidelity of our commitment to its mission and values.

We thank You for calling us to this community of research, learning, and scholarship; for the opportunities it presents us to encounter You in persons, in ideas, and experiences; for the way our engagement in this community hones our minds and urges us to transform our world through acts of service and justice.

May the message we hear today both encourage and challenge us. May it call us to support one another in our ongoing efforts, so that our work together may more and more reflect Your deepest desires for the ministry of this university and for the persons who form this community. And to this we all say:

Amen.

*Sheila Carney, RSM is Special Assistant to the President for Mercy Heritage and Service at Carlow University, Pittsburgh, PA.*

### Prayer for the End of the Academic Year

*Sheila Carney, RSM*

God of all our days, we gather at the conclusion of this academic year conscious of Your companionship and grateful for our blessings. We thank You for the ways we have developed through this year—each of us personally and professionally—and for the ways in which our university has grown as we strive together to fulfill the mission entrusted to us. We pray today for our graduates, that they will carry our values with them into future endeavors; we pray for all those whose lives now take them in other directions. As one year leads to the next, we also remember the incoming students, new faculty and staff who will join this community over the coming months. With faith in Your continuous care and protection, we entrust all to You.

Amen.

*Sheila Carney, RSM is Special Assistant to the President for Mercy Heritage and Service at Carlow University, Pittsburgh, PA.*

## Prayer for an Award Ceremony

*Carol Ziegler, SND*

God of love, tonight we celebrate Your gifts in each of our lives and Your faithfulness in the life of *name of recipient*. Faithfulness, the standing with and standing by in good times and challenging times, is a hallmark of Your relationship with the human family and with each of us.

Tonight we celebrate the faithfulness of *name of recipient, name of institution graduate, wife, mother,* and generous supporter. Thank You for *his or her* attentive and faithful response to Your call. Thank You for *name of recipient's* loving and constantly growing circle of family and friends, many of whom are gathered here tonight.

Bless our meal. Bless those who prepared and now serve that meal. We remain mindful of our responsibility to share our energy and our resources with others. We thank You as we do so often in the name of Jesus Christ, our Lord.

Amen.

*Carol Ziegler, SND is Special Assistant for Mission Effectiveness at Notre Dame College, South Euclid, OH.*

## prayer TWELVE
● ● ● ● ● ●

**Prayer for Matriculation**

*Sheila Carney, RSM*

Our good God, we ask You to watch over the class of _____. May they embrace this new experience of education with all the opportunities and challenges it presents. May they be inspired by our values and motivated in their response. As we stand with them today at the commencement of their university career, we ask that You hold them in Your generous care until, strengthened and empowered by their membership in this community, they cross another threshold into a world that awaits their skill and their service. We ask this in confidence, for we know that You hear and attend to our prayers.

Amen.

*Sheila Carney, RSM is Special Assistant to the President for Mercy Heritage and Service at Carlow University, Pittsburgh, PA.*

# additional references

■■■■■■■■■■■■■■■■■■■■■■

## Electronic

1. *The Application of Ex corde Ecclesiae for the United States*, National Conference of Catholic Bishops. http://old.usccb.org/bishops/application_of_excordeecclesiae.shtml

2. *Ex corde Ecclesiae*, Pope John Paul II. http://www.vatican.va/holy_father/john_paul_ii/apost_constitutions/documents/hf_jp-ii_apc_15081990_ex-corde-ecclesiae_en.html

3. *Gaudium et Spes*, Pope Paul VI. http://www.vatican.va/archive/hist_councils/ii_vatican_council/documents/vat-ii_cons_19651207_gaudium-et-spes_en.html

4. United States Conference of Catholic Bishops website: www.usccb.org

5. Vatican website: www.vatican.va

## Print

1. Association of Catholic Colleges and Universities, Association of Jesuit Colleges and Universities, and Association of Governing Boards of Universities and Colleges. (2003). *Mission and Identity: A Handbook for Trustees of Catholic Colleges and Universities*. Washington, DC: Association of Catholic Colleges and Universities.

2. Galligan-Stierle, Michael, ed. (2005). *Promising Practices: Collaboration Among Catholic Bishops and University Presidents*. Fairfield, CT: Sacred Heart University Press.

3. Pope John Paul II. (1990). *Ex corde Ecclesiae: On Catholic Universities*. Vatican City: Typis Polyglottis Vaticanis.

4. United States Conference of Catholic Bishops. (2000). *The Application of Ex corde Ecclesiae for the United States*. Washington, DC: United States Conference of Catholic Bishops.

5. Vatican Council II. (1996). "*Gaudium et Spes* [Pastoral constitution on the Church in the modern world]." In *The Vatican Collection: The Conciliar and Postconciliar Documents*, Vol. 1, edited by Austin Flannery, pp. 903–1001. Northport, NY: Costello.

# about ACCU

## Association of Catholic Colleges and Universities (ACCU)

*www.accunet.org*

### Mission

The ASSOCIATION OF CATHOLIC COLLEGES AND UNIVERSITIES, founded in 1899, serves as the collective voice of U.S. Catholic higher education. Through programs and services, the association strengthens and promotes the Catholic identity and mission of its member institutions so that all associated with Catholic higher education can contribute to the greater good of the world and the Church.

ACCU serves its member campuses in a number of timely and critical ways, helping foster vibrant Catholic identity at member institutions, supporting cooperation among members, and responding to emerging member needs.

### The Voice of Catholic Higher Education

- Representation of member colleges and universities with the White House, the U.S. Department of Education, and the Washington Higher Education Secretariat
- Ongoing conversations with Church officials
- Regular interaction with media, both secular and religious
- Frequent communications on critical developments related to Catholic higher education

### Support for Catholic Mission and Identity

- Full-day conference devoted to helping mission officers strengthen Catholic mission and identity on campus
- Catholic mission and identity leadership formation program for first- and second-year presidents
- Opportunity to attend the Rome Seminar and engage with key representatives within the Holy See
- Materials on strengthening Catholic identity
- Consultations with national office staff on best practices

### Publications and Research

- The peer-reviewed, semi-annual *Journal of Catholic Higher Education*
- The quarterly electronic newsletter *Update*

### A Platform for Networking and Exposure Among Peers

- Opportunities to connect and collaborate with leaders of Catholic higher education institutions
- Publicity for job openings
- Inclusion in a searchable database of scholarly centers and institutes
- Access to mailing labels of other member campuses

Made in the USA
Middletown, DE
23 May 2015